A *DOCTRINE &*

Reading Scripture
for
Living the Christian Life

Edited by

Bernard Treacy OP

with

Frances M. Young, J. Cecil McCullough

and Thomas Brodie OP

DOMINICAN PUBLICATIONS

First published (2009) by
Dominican Publications
42 Parnell Square
Dublin 1

ISBN 1-905604-12-2

978-1-905604-12-8

British Library Cataloguing in Publications Data.
A catalogue record for this book is available
from the British Library.

Cover design by Bill Bolger

Printed in Ireland by
Naas Printing Ltd
Naas, Co. Kildare.

This book is issued to subscribers to *Doctrine & Life*
for November and December 2009
at no extra cost to their pre-paid subscriptions.

It may be cited as
Doctrine & Life,
vol. 59, nos. 9 and 10,
November and December 2009.

Contents

C. Application and Assessment

Introduction

THE DEVELOPMENT among Catholics of interest in Bible study and in living by a Bible-based spirituality has been one of the fruits of the reforms flowing from Vatican II. And this development is something Catholics, happily, have been able to share with Christians of other traditions – all flowing from the ecumenical welcome given to the Constitution *Dei Verbum.*

The recovery of the ancient practice of *lectio divina* – described once as a prayerful reading of Scripture leading towards unifying our lives within the framework of God's salvation plan – has been at the heart of this renewed biblical spirituality. Cardinal Carlo Maria Martini, Fr Carlos Mesters, and Fr Michel de Verteuil have been among its most prominent advocates. For many years, Fr Brendan Clifford, O.P., following the example of Fr de Verteuil, laboured quietly at introducing individuals and groups to the value of this approach. When the Dominican Biblical Institute was set up in Limerick in 2000 and he was appointed to its staff, the promotion of *lectio divina* became one of its core activities. At his prompting, the Institute made *lectio divina* a central topic at a conference it organised on how Scripture is read in the Church and by the individual Christian. As the ecumenical team who worked on the conference explain in their Preface, the focus was on how to build bridges between different styles of Bible study – the academic style designed to uncover how a text developed and to present its meaning in its own era, and more meditative styles, designed to enhance the spiritual life.

We at Dominican Publications are glad to have the opportunity to bring out the papers of the Biblical Institute conference in book form. We trust that making them available to a wider public will contribute to advancing the renewed interest in biblical spirituality which is enriching so many people's Christian lives, and to facilitating the ecumenical understanding that is now such a welcome part of biblical study.

Bernard Treacy OP, *editor,* Doctrine & Life

Preface

MANY students, teachers and readers experience a sharp division between discussions of biblical matters in the classroom and the challenge of applying the Bible to daily life. To address this division a diverse team came together in Limerick, Ireland, and their contributions have now been edited by an ecumenical team.

The result is a book which is primarily about promoting dialogue between two opposing tendencies in biblical studies, between focusing on the past, a tendency associated especially with modern historical criticism, and focusing on the present, an approach linked to various forms of reader-response, and especially to meditative application to life – a practice sometimes known by its ancient name, sacred reading, *lectio divina*.

In the first part of the book (Section A) the problem is set out by academician/preacher Frances Young. She summarizes the central methods of interpretation, ancient and modern, and proposes a framework which respects both and benefits from both. In response to Frances Young, academician/preacher/bishop Martin Drennan develops her idea of Scripture as transformative and outlines the nature of biblical spirituality.

Section B surveys ways of dealing with the challenge in diverse situations and countries – in the academic setting (Seamus O'Connell), in the parish (Chris Hayden), in the West Indies (Pat Elie), and in Brazil and in face of fundamentalism (Carlos Mesters). Finally, in a major survey of much of the challenge to apply the Bible responsibly, Ludger Feldkämper draws on his massive experience to summarize the work of teachers as diverse as Carlo Maria Martini (Rome/Milan) and Maura Cho (Korea/USA).

Section C consists of contributions from an Italian bishop and a Northern Ireland Protestant, providing an example of how to apply a specific text to life; reflecting on the conference and its ecumenical implications.

Thomas Brodie OP, Frances M. Young, J. Cecil McCullough

Ways of Reading the Bible

Can we relativise the historico-critical method and rediscover a biblical spirituality?

FRANCES M. YOUNG

I N THIS PAPER I shall attempt three things. I shall outline the methods of biblical interpretation that have dominated the modern (as distinct from the past and the post-modern) period, remarking on the value and importance of the so-called 'historico-critical' challenge to traditional interpretation, as well as its pitfalls.[1] I intend to provide comparison and contrast by looking at the methods of interpretation used in the early Church, briefly indicating its legacy in the medieval 'four senses' of Scripture.[2] I propose to develop a model of interpretation[3] whereby we can hold this together with the historico-critical method, with benefits from both, while defining *lectio divina* against this background, and offering a doctrinal model of Holy Scripture which could undergird this.[4]

So I shall not suggest that we discard the historico-critical method,

1. In this section I will eschew footnotes, since it simply summarises for the general reader already well-known material.
2. In this section I am reproducing and adapting my own work published elsewhere, e.g. 'The Rhetorical Schools and Their Influence on Patristic Exegesis,' in Rowan Williams (ed.), *The Making of Orthodoxy, Essays in Honour of Henry Chadwick*, 1989, Cambridge, Cambridge University Press, pp. 182-199; 'Interpretative Genres and the Inevitability of Pluralism', in *JSNT* 59 (1995), pp. 93-110; *Biblical Exegesis and the Formation of Christian Culture*, 1997, Cambridge, Cambridge University Press. 'The Interpretation of Scripture', in *The First Christian Theologians*, ed. G. R. Evans, 2004, Oxford, Blackwell Publishing, pp. 24-38. For detailed footnotes these should, for the most part, be consulted.
3. This was originally published in 'The Pastorals and the Ethics of Reading,' *JSNT* 45 (1992), pp. 105-120.
4. This has previously been outlined in *The Art of Performance: towards a Theology of Holy Scripture*, 1990, London, Darton Longman and Todd.

Frances M. Young, a Methodist preacher, is emeritus professor of Scripture, University of Birmingham, U.K. Her publications include *Biblical Exegesis and the Formation of Christian Culture*.

but rather put it into relation with past approaches so that it can be transcended.

I. THE HISTORICO-CRITICAL METHOD

A number of things contributed to the rise of the modern historico-critical method.

In the fifteenth century the Renaissance and the work of great scholars like Erasmus reminded people that the word of Scripture did not come in the Latin of the Vulgate, but rather Greek was the language of the New Testament, and what Christians call the Old Testament was originally in Hebrew. As printing superseded manuscripts, questions about the differences between the hand-written witnesses became significant, and the attempt to find what lay behind these differences, so as to provide printed editions of the pristine, uncontaminated original, became paramount. So one big factor was the drive to get back to the original and pare away all the mistakes and misinterpretations that had accumulated over the centuries.

This has to be important. We all know that we cannot make things mean what we like: we argue over meaning in everyday life, sometimes because we have misheard, sometimes because we have not grasped the point the other person was trying to make; occasionally the person will say, 'I said so-and-so but I really meant so-and-so'. In other words language carries meaning, and we cannot arbitrarily attribute meanings to words or sentences which do not fit them. To understand something requires the establishment of exactly what was said in the original language, and that involves acquiring the expertise to do it.

A second factor was the rise of what has been called the 'romantic' view of what happens when one reads a text. In the nineteenth century it was famously described as 'thinking the author's thoughts after him'. So primacy was given to authorial intention – the meaning lay in what the author had in mind when he wrote it.

So in reading any text from the ancient world, the Greek and Latin classics as well as the Bible, the first thing was to grapple with the question what was in the author's mind. In the case of Scripture this meant establishing who the author was, with the time or occasion of the writing and how it fitted into the author's situation and purposes, so as to discern the original meaning. Dating, biographical details, events and relationships would provide clues to authorial intention; so reconstruction of the original situation was fundamental.

This too has to be important. In our everyday arguments about meaning we sometimes find a person saying, 'You misunderstand – I was referring to something else'. We certainly will better understand what we read if we know something of the circumstances. Paul provides the most obvious example: he was writing letters to his congregations about all kinds of problems in the churches, and if we can reconstruct what was going on we shall get his point much better.

Then alongside this was the rise of what has been called 'historical consciousness': that is, the sense that back then was not the same as now. Another famous quotation is 'The past is a foreign country'. People grow up within a culture which shapes their whole way of thinking, and people think differently in different cultures. That applies not just across the globe in different areas, but across time in different periods. So uncovering that other world where the author lived, becoming acquainted with the author's context, cultural assumptions, influences, sources, through studying parallel literature which could illuminate what the author might have meant – all this became crucial, and it remains so.

There is a lot more to translation than simply substituting the words of a different language, since all kinds of resonances and assumptions are carried for people whose culture it is. You need to enter the biblical world with an informed imagination. Here, the developing science of archaeology had a big contribution to make, setting the material in the Hebrew Bible in the wider culture of the Ancient Near East as it was rediscovered through the unearthing and decipherment of hieroglyphs and cuneiform.

But the sense of the 'otherness' of the past also meant asking whether the religious and theological ideas were really the same as ours, and it encouraged attempts to make implausible narratives fit modern understanding. For example, scientific developments challenged the possibility of many of the miracle-stories in the Bible: so sceptics made hay with the credulity of believers, and serious scholars looked for cultural explanations – 'What really happened was so-and-so, but people back then didn't understand the world the way we do, so they imagined it happened in a way we cannot believe it did.' The past is a foreign country.

One can immediately see how these three factors would drive the enterprise that has been called the 'Quest for the Historical Jesus' – the Jesus of History had to be distinguished from the Christ of Faith, so that we could uncover what really happened. We can also see how the historico-critical method could enable theologians to meet the scientific challenges to the Bible's accounts of creation – these stories came from a pre-scientific culture, and reflect the understanding of the Ancient Near East. These are just two of the consequences which have caused controversy and still do, in the deep divisions between those called liberals and fundamentalists.

The important thing to notice is that scholars of both those opposing camps are in fact stuck with the historico-critical method: the original meaning, or the literal meaning understood in those terms, is the starting-point. The particular kind of literal fundamentalism that is around today in conservative Christianity is the child of modernity. It is not traditional interpretation. It is concerned with the factuality of the events behind the text, and shares this with so-called liberal scholars. All alike agree that the original meaning is the only valid meaning. It is, we might say, an entirely archaeological approach.

The biblical scholarship of the nineteenth and twentieth centuries has been dominated by these assumptions. To understand the Bible properly you need to be expert in the languages and cultures of the all the different periods from which the biblical books come, which means even the experts become narrow specialists in particular bits of the Bible, and ordinary readers are dependent on the experts if they are going to understand the Scriptures. That understanding means understanding what the texts meant originally, and it is not the job of the experts to tell us what it might mean for us now. This latter problem has given rise to 'hermeneutics', which explores the philosophy of how texts from another world can mean anything to us in ours.

But despite all these problems with the method, it has had enormously important fruits. It has meant, for example, that Jews and Christians could join together in a common enterprise as they tried to understand the same texts in their historical context. And since Vatican II Roman Catholic scholars have been able to join in the same project on the same terms. So it has been ecumenically important that there has been a common understanding of what the appropriate methods of interpretation are. It has also enabled study of the Bible to be conducted in the public domain, and its meaning debated in the academic world, without reference to any prior commitment or belief.

However, many of these assumptions are breaking down in what has been called the 'post-modern' context, and their disadvantages are becoming clearer. We turn to our second objective – to outline by comparison and contrast the approach to biblical interpretation found in the Church Fathers.

II. BIBLICAL EXEGESIS IN THE FATHERS

Patristic biblical interpretation was largely dismissed by the modern historico-critics because in their terms the Fathers really had no historical sense, and their so-called allegory allowed any meaning to be read into the text. Yet, paradoxically, commentaries still cover much the same ground as they did back then, though often with rather different outcomes.

It is important to realise first how much more like a school than a religion the early Church was. The apologists had to respond to the charge that Christians were atheists because they had no temples, offered no sacrifices, in fact did nothing recognisably religious. They were more like philosophers, with teachings (= dogmas, doctrines) about the way the world is and how you should live your life (metaphysics and ethics); they gathered round teachers to read texts and interpret them.

Reading Texts at School: the Origins of the Commentary

We need to understand the physical reality: handwritten copies in the form of scrolls or codices, with no punctuation or even word-division, though some paragraph distinctions. Did all the copies in the classroom have the same wording? Had the text been tampered with? How were the words to be divided where there was ambiguity and different possibilities? 'Correct reading precedes interpretation', writes one ancient textbook. The first stage, then, was to establish the text – and as we have seen this was recovered in early modern biblical scholarship as a primary issue. The Fathers are aware of these contingencies and at crucial points they are discussed.[5]

In the ancient world the written text was regarded rather like a tape is now – it was a recording of speech. Reading was generally aloud rather than in people's heads, and the object was recitation of the text, a kind of re-play. Sometimes tone of voice determines meaning which is not indicated in the written form: a statement could become a question if read differently, or it might be ironical – in other words it might actually imply the opposite of what it said. Such things are often discussed in commentaries, and, similarly, doubtful texts were discussed by the Fathers.

Then there is grammar, and this involved parsing, vocabulary, and indentifying figures of speech. Parsing words could show how they fit together in sentences – commentators still discuss such things where the original language is unclear or ambiguous. In vocabulary it was important toexplain ancient words no longer in everyday usage, or words with specialised senses in a particular body of literature: in the schools Homer presented problems, in the Church the translationese of the Septuagint – in both cases exegetes would collect lists of instances and examples to show how the words were used in the relevant body of text, and commentators still do this.

It was alos essentila to identify figures of speech, such as irony, but also metaphor, parable, hyperbole, and other techniques adopted to catch attention or reinforce the point. These were called 'tropes' or 'turns' of language. They remain current in our everyday speech: my children could always play with the non-literal character of language, teasing with a phrase like 'Mum's climbing up the wall'. In similar vein, what the Fathers were clear about is that you cannot do things like taking 'God is my Rock' according to the letter, or literally, and worship the Standing Stone on the hill.

The ancients also loved etymology, explaining the meanings of words by analysing their supposed roots – a good example occurs in the New Testament: the Hebrew roots of the name Melchisedek mean King of Righteousness, and he was King of Salem = Peace (though it

---

5. Quintilian, *Institutio Oratoria* I. iv-ix provides a general account of what is summarised here.

was an alternative name for Jerusalem). In the Epistle to the Hebrews this initiates a reading of the Genesis passage as pointing to our High Priest, Jesus Christ. Now we can see how the same techniques of identifying grammatical characteristics in the language produce different outcomes: the modern interpreter would keep Melchisedek firmly placed in his historical (or perhaps pre-historical and legendary) place, while making similar comments about the meaning of his name. Allegory may grow out of linguistic analysis. For language always points beyond itself.

So far we have looked at the way they attended to the wording, and their recognition that the words point beyond themselves. The phrase we might translate as 'literal' did not mean 'literal' in the modern sense, but rather this careful attention to the 'letter' – to the nature of the language being used. All this would be called *to grammaticon*.

The next stage was called *to historikon*.

We have to grasp that this did not mean 'historical' in our sense. The Greek word means 'investigation', and this implied enquiry concerning unexplained allusions in the text to myths or well-known stories, characters, events, heroes, legends, facts of geography or history – explanatory notes of all kinds. This potentially distorts the reading of the text by distracting from what the text is about to what the commentator finds problematic or interesting – Origen offers pages of comment on the 'pearl':[6] he writes down everything he could find out about pearls and where and how they form, showing off his learning, but hardly increasing our grasp of what Jesus was getting at when he spoke of the pearl of great price.

Among the Fathers, Origen may be identified as the first really professional biblical scholar who produced commentaries. These have been described as 'a strange mixture of philological, textual, historical, etymological notes and theological and philosophical observations'.[7] Exactly so. Commentaries are still a bit like that because they arise out of following through a text providing notes and explanations as they go along in order to explain some difficult point in wording or reference. Comments are problem-oriented, often taking up problem-

6. Commentary on Matthew X.7-10.
7. J. Quasten, *Patrology*, 1953, Westminster, MD, The Newman Press, II, pp. 45-48.

points discussed by earlier commentators, or noting new difficulties – there is no comment where the meaning is obvious. One ancient commentator[8] remarked that it is the job of the commentator to deal with problems, whereas the task of the preacher is to reflect on words that are perfectly clear and speak about them.

This piecemeal approach to interpretation was mitigated by paraphrase and summary. Paraphrase is a kind of interpretative translation – not word for word, but bringing out the meaning in another way (Targum would be an example); but the way something is said subtly changes its impact and possibly its meaning. Different paraphrases may bring out different nuances and different potential layers of meaning. I said earlier language carries meaning and you cannot make it mean what you like, and yet language is not rigidly finite either. We may not be able to determine a single definitive meaning. Exegesis is a process of substitution, but that very substitution produces slightly different tones and senses.

Summary derives from the ancient schools who made a distinction between the subject-matter and the wording/style: the wording was the clothing in which the subject-matter was dressed. They recognised there were many different ways in which the same thing could be said, and often insisted that the style should be appropriate to the subject. As they read texts they sought to discern the 'hypothesis' or argument underlying the outer dress of the style. So ancient commentaries, like modern commentaries, would summarise the argument of each section, or the text as a whole. This helps to counteract the piecemeal and problem-oriented character of commentaries.

In these ways, modern commentaries are very like ancient ones. But now we can see some of the differences: they had a very different approach to coherence, sequence and structure, found different things problematic and had very different interests. The modern historico-critic spots incoherences and analyses inconsistencies in order to read between the lines and reach theories about the facts or history behind the text; the ancient reader was usually concerned with moral, spiritual or dogmatic meaning and worried when texts seemed to contradict themselves doctrinally: how could Jesus Christ both say, 'My Father is

---

8. Theodore of Mopsuestia, Introduction to his Commentary on John.

greater than I' and 'I and the Father are one'?

In other words, exegetical methods are not dissimilar, but interests are, and so different meanings emerge. This observation is confirmed by an article by Kenneth Hagan,[9] writing of a very different time, the sixteenth century. He shows that there were three forms of interpretation: 'sacred page' (the monastic interest in Scripture as intended to guide the pilgrim's journey to God); 'sacred doctrine' (the scholastic interest in understanding the faith of the Church); and 'sacred letter' (the humanistic tradition begun by Erasmus whereby the Bible, along with other literature, was read for its wisdom, leading to piety, morality and justice, and so a better society, better Church, better education, better government). The difference lay in the different interests in what the Bible said.

So what were the interests of the early Church? To deduce right doctrine from Scripture, especially in the face of heretics; to spell out the right way of life for Christian believers – ethics, ascetic ideals, etc., and to find maps for the spiritual journey of the soul. In other words, they were less interested in the 'material', 'earthly', 'historical or 'factual' meaning than the theological or spiritual meaning.

This too had a background in the schools. The great philosopher Plato had attacked Homer and the poets for the immorality of the stories; so people had to show how to find moral lessons in the texts which formed the backbone of education. By the time the early Church was doing similar things with the Bible, philosophers were finding all their doctrine in Homer by allegorical interpretation.

For the Fathers, the Bible was the Word of God for the Church and its people NOW.

They believed that God had accommodated the transcendent divine self to our human level not only in the incarnation but also in the language of Scripture. So how did they get to this deeper meaning?

- From linguistic analysis, metaphor, etc. (as already indicated), and cross-referencing different scriptural passages that use the same wording

9 .K. Hagan, 'What Did the Term Commentarius mean to Sixteenth-Century Theologians?' in I. Backus and F. Higman (ed.), *Théorie et pratique de l'exégèse: Actes du troisième colloque international sur l'Histoire de l'exégèse biblique au XVI siècle* (Genève, 32 aout–2 septembre 1988), 1990, Geneva, Libraire Droz.

- From prophetic oracles and riddles, assumed to be in code which had to be unpacked
- From exemplary actions/models – Job was a 'type' of patience, for example
- From puzzles (*aporiai*) – for Origen the difference between John's Gospel and the others was not a historical puzzle, but a theological opportunity

From all of these allegory was developed: so they got to the classic interpretation of the Song of Songs in terms of the love between Christ and the Church, or the soul of the believer; while Gregory of Nyssa's *Life of Moses* shows how the journey of the soul follows the same pattern as the stories of Moses' life. And there developed a symbol system allowing one always to interpret Jerusalem as referring to the Church, Joshua as a 'type' of Christ, etc.

There was a reaction against allegory in the fourth century, yet the anti-allegorist was also finding 'types' and 'symbols', morals and doctrines in the Scriptures – they just avoided certain arbitrary methods of decoding associated with allegory.

All of the Fathers were trying to discern the underlying eternal meaning intended by the Holy Spirit, rather than the historical factual meaning which has dominated modern interpretation.

So what did they think the Bible was all about? What was the subject-matter behind the wording?

The Subject-matter of Scripture – Christ

Here, it should be said, 'Christ' covers a range of things – obviously the incarnation, but also the 'Body of Christ', that is the Church, the sacraments, Christians, their moral life, their salvation and final destiny, and so on.

The view that the whole of Scripture refers to Christ arose very quickly and was consolidated in various ways.

Already in the New Testament there is the assumption that Christ fulfils the prophecies. The Dead Sea Scrolls and apocalyptic literature from the period show that many Jewish groups practised the 'prophetic' reading of Scripture, and for Christians this meant that Christ was there in the Law and the Prophets and the Psalms and the Wisdom-books. Prophetic interpretation often treated the Scriptures as collections of riddling oracles, and applied individual texts to particular events – the New Testament showed the way, and the Fathers developed it.

In Jewish tradition of the time we can trace the expectation that future salvation has been prefigured in the past as recounted in Scripture. So events of the Exodus were to be replayed. In the New Testament the classic example is the miracle of the feeding in the wilderness, which is shown, implicitly in the Synoptic Gospels, explicitly in John's Gospel, to be the fulfilment of the manna in the desert. The Fathers developed this so that the crossing of the Red Sea prefigured baptism, the Passover the Eucharist, and so on.

So Scripture was taken to have a symbolic meaning throughout; it was always pointing beyond itself.

In the third century the scholarship of Origen took up all these traditions and developed them into the spiritual meaning of Scripture. The meaning was veiled until Christ came and revealed what it was all about. *Aporiai*, the puzzles and difficulties of Scripture, were deliberately put there by the Holy Spirit to provoke the reader into discerning this deeper meaning intended by the Spirit. Progress in the spiritual journey was related to different levels of reading: the literal meaning was often important – you cannot ignore 'Thou shalt not murder'. But the literal meaning was there for the simple, for the beginners; moral and spiritual meanings were for those who were making progress, and they were discerned by allegory. The feeding of the multitude was a symbol of spiritual feeding by God's Word.

Origen's allegory sometimes produced many different interpretations of the same passage; he outlined a theory of three levels of meaning, but in practice offered multiple meanings in basically two modes – the literal and the spiritual. Nevertheless we can see in the Fathers, as they responded to his lead, the elements that would lead to the medieval analysis of four senses of Scripture: the literal, the allegorical, the moral and the anagogical. To explain briefly: the literal sense teaches what happened, allegory what you are to believe, the moral sense what you are to do, anagogy where you are going – there is a spiritual progression through levels of meaning.[10]

---

10. *Littera gesta docet, quid credas allegoria, moralia quid agas, quo tendas anagogia.* Quoted in A. Louth, *Discerning the Mystery*, 1983, Oxford, Clarendon Press, p. 116

Even with the fourth century reaction against allegory Christ remained the subject-matter: typology and prophecy were not rejected, and *theoria*, or insight, was encouraged – deeper moral and doctrinal meanings were assumed to be what Scripture offered.

All of this is foreign to the historico-critical approach to the Bible, which, amongst other things, would set the prophecies in the time of the prophets, rather than assuming they were predictions of events centuries later. Some modern scholars, such as Daniélou, have tried to reclaim typology,[11] suggesting that the consistent patterning of events derives from God's providence, and so history, especially salvation-history, is reflected in this. But that approach reinforces the contrast – the primacy of history for Daniélou and modern interpreters, over against what held primacy for the early Church, namely, to discern true doctrine and derive moral and spiritual benefit from reading Scripture.

Doctrinal Reading of Scripture

Modern interpretation regards the doctrines of the Church as future developments, not actually to be found in the texts of the New Testament. They distinguish different books of the Bible by authorship and date, even dissect particular books into sources. The Fathers argue for and then assume the unity of the Bible and the presence in Scripture of orthodox doctrine.[12] This is a fundamental difference between the approach of modern interpreters and their distant predecessors. We may look briefly at three important moments.

Irenaeus, bishop of Lyon in the second century, was faced with Gnostics who produced and used books as Scripture which are not now part of our canon, and interpreted the books which did become canonical in ways that delivered the wrong outcome - at least from Irenaeus' point of view, as well as that of developed orthodoxy. At the time the Bible was not a single book – it was technically impossible to put it all together – it was a collection of books. So which belonged to the collection?

11. Jean Daniélou, *From Shadows to Reality : Studies in the Biblical Typology of the Fathers*, 1960, London, Burns and Oates; for further discussion see my paper, 'Typology', in *Crossing the Boundaries, Essays in Biblical Interpretation in Honour of Michael D. Goulder*, ed. Stanley E. Porter, Paul Joyce and David E. Orton, Leiden, E. J. Brill, pp. 29-48.

12. For fuller discussion of the points in this section, see my previous discussions in *The Art of Performance* and *Biblical Exegesis*.

The writings of Irenaeus contain the first attempt at defining the boundaries, and the first clear outline of what constitutes the unity of the Scriptures and the criteria for interpreting them as a unity. This is contained in what he calls the 'Rule of Faith' or the 'Canon of Truth'. It is not a fixed formula and appears in several different forms in his writings, but basically it is like the creeds. It affirms one God, the Creator of all, who sent Jesus Christ to be our Saviour in fulfilment of the prophecies of the Holy Spirit, and who will bring all things to fulfilment in the end. In other words, there is an over-arching story which is the Bible's fundamental content, and you cannot read the Scriptures 'Christianly' without taking this seriously, and seeing that all the details relate to that outline.

Athanasius, bishop of Alexandria in the fourth century, was faced with the heretic Arius and his successors. To an extent not always appreciated, the interpretation of Scripture lay at the heart of the controversy. Each side appealed to particular biblical texts. One of these was Proverbs 8.22:'The Lord created me [that is, wisdom] in the beginning of his ways'.[13] Both sides assumed the text was about the pre-existent Christ, who was identified with God's Word and Wisdom. Arius deduced that Wisdom was a creature. How was Athanasius to deal with this over-literal interpretation? He argued that you have to attend to the mind/sense of Scripture as a whole, and interpret individual texts in the light of the total perspective. In this case, the Christ did become a creature in the incarnation, but was the Word of God from eternity.

Augustine, bishop of Hippo in North Africa in the late fourth and early fifth centuries, wrote a book about scriptural interpretation – its title is *On Christian Doctrine*, but that just bears out what I was saying earlier about 'doctrine' meaning teaching and the reading of texts in schools. He makes a distinction between the subject-matter (res) and the language or signs (signa) that point to it. So his first book concentrates on the subject-matter and identifies it as 'Love God and love your neighbour'. Then every detail has to be interpreted in the light of that, and if anything does not fit with that it has to be carefully

13. See further my paper 'Proverbs 8 in Interpretation (2): Wisdom Personified', in *Reading Texts, Seeking Wisdom*, ed. David F. Ford and Graham Stanton, 2003, London, SCM Press, pp. 102-115.

considered and interpreted until it does.

So to gather up the main points:

- The Fathers insisted on the unity of Scripture by contrast with modernist analysis and differentiation.
- They were primarily interested in the spiritual/moral/Christological sense rather than having the historical interest of modern interpreters.
- They had an 'external' test of how to read Scripture aright, which we can roughly identify as the 'creed' in one form or another. (One post-modern approach known as canon-criticism, tries to interpret in the light of the Bible as a whole, as the Fathers did, but fails to see that the Bible is not self-explanatory unless there is some kind of a framework.)
- They said a person had to have inspiration to read Scripture – it was not just that the text was inspired, and for Scripture to speak one had to see oneself in it, and learn from it; modern interpretation seeks to be objective rather than subjective.
- They recognised the inadequacies of human language to express the divine, and so saw the language of Scripture as symbolic of deeper meanings.
- They understood that God in his infinite divine grace had accommodated the divine self to our level both in the incarnation and in the language of Scripture.

III. A MODEL OF INTERPRETATION FOR TODAY

In the latter part of the twentieth century scholarly interpretation of Scripture largely remained in its historico-critical phase, but some of the fundamentals of this method were also challenged.[14] The possibility of objectivity began to be questioned, given the impossibility of divesting the investigator of all presuppositions, and so was the value of an exclusively 'archaeological' approach to meaning, distancing

---

14. The following paragraphs reproduce and adapt material found in Craig Bartholomew, Scott Hahn, Robin Parry, Christopher Seitz and Al Wolters (eds.), *Canon and Biblical Interpretation*, Scripture and Hermeneutics Series vol. 7, Published by Paternoster in the UK (Milton Keynes) and Zondervan in the US (Grand Rapids), 2006. My contribution is found as Chapter 8: Jean Vanier and Frances Young, 'Towards Transformational Reading of Scripture', pp. 236-254.

the reader from the text.

Meanwhile, critical theory changed the approach to texts across the whole field of literary studies, and this began to affect biblical interpretation too. Structuralism shifted the focus away from the original 'authorial intention' – the French thinker Roland Barthes wrote a famous essay entitled, 'The Death of the Author'. Attention was given instead to analysis of the text itself: for texts might carry a surplus of meaning that the author never intended. Structuralism, however, soon gave way to interest in the reader: for texts have no reality until 're-played' through someone making sense of the black and white patterns on the paper - so the reader's contribution became paramount. It was then noticed that traditions of reading are formed in 'reading communities', that texts can acquire authority and 'create worlds' – so, for example, the Bible had reinforced social orders which included slavery and patriarchy. The future of the text, its potential to generate new meaning, became important for interpretation, not just its past, or its background. Meanwhile hermeneutics had been attending to questions concerning the gap between the world of ancient texts and the world of the reader.

So, one way and another the question how texts are to be read is more open now than it was 100 years ago. Then it was generally assumed that arguments, especially between liberals and conservatives, were about the 'facts behind' the text, such as questions about miracles; now arguments are often about the 'future in front of' the texts', issues such as the position of women or the acceptance of persons who are gay. So this greater openness creates uncertainty: Can we make texts mean anything we like, or are there ethical standards of reading?

Against this post-modern background I want to suggest a model[15] of the process of reading and interpreting which allows room for both scholarly research and spiritual reading, taking seriously the dynamics of objectivity and subjectivity implicit in each.

The object of rhetoric in the ancient world was to achieve persuasion or conviction (that is, *pistis*, usually translated 'faith' in a New

---

15. This model is a development of the work of James L. Kinneavy, *Greek Rhetorical Origins of Christian Faith*, 1987, Oxford, Oxford University Press; it has been previously published – see notes 3 and 13.

Testament context). Three things were required for this:

- The *ethos* of the author/speaker. The author's character and life-style had to be such as to inspire trust in his integrity and authority – in other words, should carry conviction.
- The *logos*. The argument, narrative, discourse of the speech/text had to be logical, reasonable, convincing.
- The *pathos* of the audience. If the readers/hearers were not swayed by the author and the argument – if there was no response – then the whole thing was ineffective and unconvincing.

Conviction depended on the dynamic interplay of author/orator, text/speech and reader/audience. These three elements were inter-acting, and as it happens they are the three which modern and post-modern criticism have successively prioritised – they need to work together, as in Figure 1.

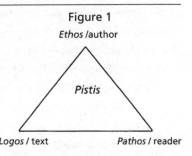

Figure 1
Ethos /author
Pistis
Logos / text   *Pathos* / reader

But in the case of Scripture, we can see a series of different dynamic triangles. The author may be identified, say, as Paul, writing a letter to his converts in Corinth (figure 2)

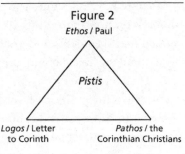

Figure 2
Ethos / Paul
Pistis
Logos / Letter   *Pathos* / the
to Corinth   Corinthian Christians

But if that is the case, 'we' are not the intended readers, and there is no way in which exactly that original situation can be recreated.

Alternatively, we may identify the author as the Holy Spirit, ourselves as believers in the context of liturgy – part of the Church universal over time and space, and the material as an extract from the timeless, canonical 'Word of God' (figure 3).

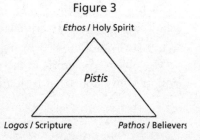

Figure 3
Ethos / Holy Spirit
Pistis
Logos / Scripture   *Pathos* / Believers

This is a different 'reading gen-re' with a very different dynamic, and it never exists in a 'pure' sense; for we carry over the previous dynamic triangle, knowing that the text was shaped by human history and by particular circumstances, and that we are too – we do not read Holy Scripture now in the same way as believers in the Middle Ages. Scripture is the divine Word in human words – it is incarnational, and the point of Scripture is transformation: it is meant to carry conviction and change people's lives. In every generation and in different cultures, particularities somehow carry the eternal Word of God. Somehow, we need to keep both dynamic triangles in play, and the concern of the 'modern' scholar, to be 'objective', and the concern of the believer, 'subjectively' to hear the Word of God, are both valid and true to the nature of Scripture.

So our model necessitates recognising the involvement of the reader when it comes to the interpretation of Scripture. The reader cannot simply make the text mean anything he likes – he/she must respect the 'otherness' of the text. On the other hand, we can discern a legitimate place for the believer approaching the texts for insight and spiritual transformation; for it is new insight that the believer seeks from the texts – a mirror reflecting back his/her own prejudices is a danger, but not necessarily the outcome: rather the text stands over against the reader, challenging and calling into a new future. Always the reader interacts with author and text, and ideally is changed by the process - for the point of Scripture is transformation.

What of Lectio Divina?

So in the light of all this, how would we define *lectio divina*? Can we hold it alongside the historico-critical method? And can we offer a doctrine of holy Scripture which would justify this?

By *lectio divina* I understand the process of reading oneself into the text so as to come away changed. Cardinal Martini put the same thing in a slightly different way when speaking at the *Dei Verbum* Congress 2005 on the importance of the Vatican II statement on Holy Scripture.[16] What is meant by *lectio divina* is 'devotional reading', 'spiritual' in the sense that it is done under the impulse of the Holy Spirit, in the context of the Church. It is 'prayerful reading', allowing us to 'unify our lives within the framework of [God's] salvation plan'. The 'spiritual and

16. Published in the *Bulletin of the Catholic Biblical Federation* 76/77 (2005), pp. 33-38.

meditative experience' of *lectio divina* may not be 'strictly exegetical'. The Bible is to be treated as if it were a 'Someone who speaks to the one reading and stirs in him a dialogue of faith and hope, or repentance, of intercession, of self-offering...'

Martini emphasizes three moments: *lectio, meditatio, contemplatio.* Reading means reading as if for the first time, seeking to discover the key words, the characters, the actions, the context, both in Scripture and in one's own time. What is this text saying? Meditating means reflection on the message of the text, its permanent values, the coordinates of the divine activity it makes known. What is this text saying to us? Contemplation points to the most personal moment of the *lectio divina*, when 'I enter into dialogue with One who is speaking to me through this text and through the whole of Scripture.' *Lectio divina* is 'prayer born of a reading of the Bible under the action of the Holy Spirit'.

This might imply freeing the Bible as God's Word from the expertise of Church leaders and clergy, and indeed from the expertise of scholars: a lay person's simple reading may discern more directly the core of what the Word of God is about. Nevertheless, we should note that Martini, just like the Fathers, puts it in the context of Church: 'in the footprints of the great ecclesial tradition, in the context of all the truths of faith and in communion with the pastors of the Church'.

As for the expertise of scholars, let me give an example of how a little historical knowledge can sharpen the message of the text for us today. The parable of the Good Samaritan was not simply about the kindness of strangers: Samaritans had no dealings with Jews (Jn 4:9), although they had the books of Moses in common and originally derived from the Twelve Tribes of Israel. They were historically close, and yet different in ethnicity and religion, hostile to one another (like Jews, Christians and Muslims; like the various peoples of the former Yugoslavia). Jesus was challenging people (i) to see the goodness of those they hated and mistrusted and regarded as heretics; (ii) to see the lack of goodness in those who rigidly obeyed religious rules (neither the priest nor the Levite could carry out their duties if they had touched a corpse, and that was why they passed by). To pick up the challenges of the parable, we need such information. So we do need to honour the expertise of scholars and Church leaders, alongside engaging in our own prayerful meditation of the text.

The theology that could undergird this is a view of Scripture that acknowledges that it is in two natures: there is the human historical reality that these texts were composed by human beings in the dialectic they used at the time and limited by the ideas and knowledge of the time, and the texts were then subject to the chances and changes of constant copying and translation; and there is the divine reality that the Word of God is alive and active – it cuts like any double-edged sword and slips through the place where the soul is divided from the spirit or joints from the marrow; it can judge the secret emotions and thoughts (Heb 4:12).

The Word of God was incarnate for our sake in the human Jesus; the Word of God is inscribed for our sake in the word of this collection of ancient books. This view of Scripture not only parallels the incarnation, but also other core doctrines of the faith, such as the real presence in the Eucharist. As the human Jesus had weaknesses and was vulnerable on earth, yet in him we see God, so Scripture is earthly and limited, yet 'teaching solidly, faithfully and without error that truth which God wanted put into sacred writings for the sake of our salvation' (*Dei Verbum*). To realise this we need the disciplined expertise of the historico-critical method alongside *lectio divina*.

Transformation through *Lectio Divina*

A response to Frances Young's paper

✠ MARTIN DRENNAN

T HROUGH THE PRACTICE of *lectio divina* we want to engage
with the word of God in a way that facilitates the transformation
of our lives. Transformation is not inevitable. Change happens if we
put in place the elements needed to bring change about. In praying
with the Scriptures the quality of the relationship between the person
praying and the Lord is crucial.

Frances has thrown considerable light on the value of scholarly
insights. In our practice of *lectio* we ask, what is this passage saying? A
rich appreciation of the Scripture text gives it a chance to speak to us
with greater impact, e.g., an understanding of the biblical use of the
image of salt. We think of salt as that which preserves and gives flavour
to food. In biblical times salt had another use, that of extracting certain
chemicals so that fire could catch. Salt was used with poor quality fire
material in a land where wood is scarce. You are the salt of the earth
(Mt 5:13). The mission of the Christian is to draw out the evil so that
the fire of the Spirit can catch.

There are several factors operative in our receptivity to the Scriptures, in our openness to transformation, in the ways we are changed.
It is on some of these that I wish to reflect, in the hope that they will
help to make us more open to the gift God wants to give us in prayer.
I want to begin with an illustration and then tease out some implications for our personal and communal journey in prayer.

Some years back I worked in a directed retreat with a priest who
came to prayer with a wonderful realism. Manager of the primary

✠ **Martin Drennan**, Bishop of Galway, is a former professor of Scripture at
St Patrick's College, Maynooth.

school in his parish, he found much of his time – far too much for his liking – taken up with problems around getting a new school built. He found it frustrating to have to travel to numerous meetings with architects and with the Department of Education.

I suggested to him that he spend time in prayer with the story of Abraham and Isaac (Gen 22:1-19). That piece of Scripture could be read as a story of God's providence, of how God provides. It is a story of Abraham's faith being tested and stretched to a new level of trust in God. At a subjective level you might read it as saying that there is an Isaac in every life that God asks us to let go of, but we want to hold on our cherished possession. I gave no guidance on how to read it, but let him be with the Lord and the Scriptures.

When he came back next day there were signs of relief and joy on his face. He told me that when he pondered the passage in prayer, the phrase that jumped off the page for him was 'Abraham saddled his ass'. He explained: 'I was resenting all year the time spent on going to one meeting after another. Now I see that through it all God was offering me the gift of patience, a gift to be found through keeping going every day. My resistance and frustration have melted away. The word of God has interpreted events for me and the past year now makes sense. I have been freed from my dogged resistance and I feel I now have new energy to face the future.' Scripture aims at transformation.

In that very real meeting with God, human need for help meeting the power of God's word, real change happened. In a prayerful setting the word of God was allowed to question, direct and shape this man's life, to form new attitudes. From his side all was on the agenda for God's intervention. Expectations were open to becoming realistic, memories open to being healed, ideas of God and life open to being refined, desires open to being purified. God's word spoke with powerful effect in this instance.

I want to focus, first on the word that God speaks and then on signs of the transformation he brings about.

THE WORD OF GOD

God is present in his word. The power of his word is rooted in the power of God. That word is all-powerful, it brings to pass what it promises. Gn 1 describes the creative action of that word which transforms chaos into order, into a world safe to live in, into something that is good, beautiful, deserving of awe, wonder. What God said came to pass; there was no resisting the might of his word. The prophet Jeremiah experienced the power of that word as fire, Is not my word like fire, says the Lord, like a hammer which breaks the rocks in pieces (23:29). At times the word overcomes all resistance, at other times resistance limits the effectiveness of the message. God speaks his word and awaits a response. Listening requires humility. The all-powerful word can meet evasion, indifference, stubbornness. The Scriptures have many examples of where it is spoken to hearers who are uninterested, obstinate. The hearer can close his ears, harden his heart, shut out what challenges. There are different levels of listening – listening against, listening to, and listening for,

Listening against

'But they say…..We will follow our own plans, and each of us will act according to the stubbornness of our evil will.' (Jer 18:12) God's plan to mould his people as a potter moulds the clay met with firm rejection. When people don't understand they usually resist, they listen against. Matthew records (Mt 16:22) Peter's resistance to the message of the Cross: 'this must never happen to you'. If the message is perceived as a threat, then a listening against it may well happen. No transformation results.

Listening to

Mk 8:32 reads, 'but they did not understand what he was saying and were afraid to ask him.' The disciples heard Jesus talk about the cost of discipleship, they listened to it, didn't connect and were unchanged by it. The Bible has many instances of people listening to the word and remaining unmoved and unchanged by it.

Listening for

Transformation in listening means moving beyond a listening against, a listening to, to a listening in favour of. Acts 4 records the story of the arrest, imprisonment and trial of Peter and John. The two men respond to a warning not to speak again to anyone about Jesus with, 'Whether it is right in God's sight to listen to you rather than to

God, you must judge; for we cannot keep from speaking about what we have seen and heard' (Acts 4:12-13). Conversion at the level of listening means giving priority to the voice of God and to his claims on them. Peter has come a long way from resistance to not understanding (perhaps not wanting to understand) to availability. It's a profound personal transformation.

BIBLICAL SPIRITUALITY

Through his word the risen Lord draws people into communion with him, draws them to adopt his values, his attitudes, his way of life. He seeks to shape their response to life. A spirituality that is based on the word of God has several features. It is incarnational, discerning, integrating and apostolic.

Being incarnational, it is rooted in the reality of life, never evasive of the issues thrown up in lived experience. God calls us to face reality as it is now, to engage with the stuff of life. Facing reality is the beginning of freedom. A fine example of God calling someone to name reality and deal with it is the story of Adam and Eve. God's question to Adam is, 'Where are you?' (Gen 3:9). At the time Adam was hiding among the trees in the garden, afraid to meet God. Rejection of the command of God and eating from the tree had changed relationships drastically, but Adam did not want to know. God's word invites him to take responsibility for his actions and face the new reality brought about by sin. The word of God calls for honest realism. That realism is the starting point for hope.

Discerning

The call of God is to choose life (Deut 30:19). The word of God draws us to where God has life for us. If, for instance, we face something regularly in bad mood we are not meeting God there. God calls us to peace, never to frustration. Rom 12:2 says that those turned towards God are in the best position to make good decisions, be transformed by the renewing of your minds, so that you may discern what is the will of God – what is good and acceptable and perfect. Through drawing us to the values and attitudes inculcated in his word God draws us to peace. Reflection on prayer notices where God gives peace, a peace that is enduring.

Integrating

Truth unites, falsehood divides. Integrating the past involves understanding it, taking responsibility for it, owning it and taking it into
account as fresh choices are made. In his Letter to the Philippians
(3:4-15) Paul looks back over a large section of his life, at what he
has found, forgetting what lies behind and straining forward to what
lies ahead. Mistaken judgments in the past don't hold him back now,
don't linger on in guilt. He has integrated his past, learned from
it, and presses on towards his goal in freedom. The healed wounds
don't hurt. Energy is not used up wrestling with old memories. He has
found peace. That word peace (shalom) means wholeness, integrity.
The word of God draws the features of life into unity, it gathers the
fragments together. It nourishes communion – with the Lord, with his
people, with his Church. The Holy Spirit is a Spirit of unity, enabling
the gifts of God to work in harmony, for the fruit of the Spirit is love,
joy peace. (Gal 5:22 – note that Paul says fruit not fruits). There is
struggle because of a divided heart (Gal 5:16-21), but it is a struggle
going towards victory. Victory means that the fragmentation caused
by sin is replaced by wholeness.

Apostolic

Every gift of God is for the building up of his people, it is for sharing.
One of the signs of growth in Christian maturity is a positive outlook
on life, a spirit of gratitude. I've seen it again and again in people who
listen to the word of God in prayer and can say with confidence that
thanksgiving is the normal outcome of Scriptural prayer. What flows
from it is a spirit of self-giving, a wanting to surrender oneself and
be available for the Lord. The call of Isaiah offers a fine example (Is
6:1-8). In the presence of the Lord Isaiah is profoundly aware of his
unworthiness, I am a man of unclean lips, and I live among a people
of unclean lips (Is 6:5). Then his lips are touched by a burning coal
and he hears the words, your guilt has departed and your sin is blotted
out. When the Lord asks, Whom shall I send ? The prophet replies,
Here I am; send me! In the presence of God he is transformed and
then from prayer he is sent out with a mission to a people in great
need of transformation.

Through his work in us the Lord seeks to transform us, to make us more God-like. *lectio divina* draws us to cooperation in that ongoing process of transfiguration. It invites us to notice the wonder of our own transformation, to notice the gift of God and make ever more space for him to fill us with his presence. With St. Paul we may one day be able to say, it is no longer I who live, but it is Christ who lives in me (Gal 2:20). When that happens for you, do let us know, for then Frances and I will know that our efforts at encouraging transformation through prayer have borne much fruit!

Lectio Divina: **The Challenge in the Academic Setting**

SÉAMUS O'CONNELL

LECTIO DIVINA may be described as the 'reading of a ... passage of Scripture, received as the Word of God and leading, at the prompting of the Spirit, to meditation, prayer and contemplation.'[1] By its very nature, *lectio* poses a challenge in the academy. Biblical scholarship in the academy has difficulties receiving Scripture as the Word of God and is also challenged by a reception that would lead to meditation, prayer and contemplation. Markus Bockmuehl summarizes well:

> Until not so very long ago, academic gatherings of biblical scholars witnessed regular recitations of the mantra that biblical exegetes must 'set aside their presuppositions' and read the Bible 'like any other ancient book.'[2]

The questions posed for academic theology by a reading of the Scriptures in faith – for this is what *lectio divina* is – mask more profound questions about the nature and character of theology in the academy. Its roots – both philosophical and political – are deep and lead to one of the defining questions in theological and philosophical debate:

---

1. Pontifical Biblical Commission, *The Interpretation of the Bible in the Church*, 1993, Vatican City, IV.C.2.
2. Markus Bockmuehl, 'Reason, Wisdom and the Implied Disciple of Scripture' in David F. Ford and Graham Stanton (eds.), *Reading Texts, Seeking Wisdom*, 2003, London, SCM Press, p. 53. A positive formulation is made by Sandra Schneiders: speaking of the historical reliability of the Gospel, she can maintain, 'faith does and *must* [italics mine] enter into the question of the historical reliability of the Gospel, not as a substitute for historical investigation that must be pursued as far as it can go, but as participation in a tradition that guarantees the reliability of the whole no matter how much the details come under question or elude explication.' *The Revelatory Text: Interpreting the New Testament as Sacred Scripture* (second edition), 1999, Collegeville, Liturgical Press, A Michael Glazier Book, p. 109.

Seamus O'Connell, Professor of Scripture, St Patrick's College, Maynooth, National University of Ireland, is author of *The Nature and Text-Critical Use of the Greek Old Testament Text of the Complutensian Polyglot Bible* in the series Orbis Biblicus et Orientalis.

the relation between faith and reason.[3] Acknowledging this broader and perennial question, this paper seeks to explore what *lectio divina* might have to contribute to contemporary academic biblical study. As *lectio* does not exist in a vacuum, this paper will also explore how some of the core values of *lectio* find a deep resonance of in contemporary biblical scholarship.

Working in a parish in rural Ireland in the late 1980s, I found that in contrast to Christmas, where a particular cultural support was palpable, the celebration of Easter was more of a challenge. From one member of the parish – let's call her 'Julia' – an invitation to participate in the Passion Sunday Liturgy drew the rather unexpected response: 'I hate that Mass! I hate when we have to say, "Crucify him! Crucify him!"' The story of the crucifixion had evoked a reponse in 'Julia' that an exposition of the doctrine of the atonement could never do. It caused its audience to engage with it. While this is a pastoral context, the identical dynamics of the Gospel are at work in more recent academic approaches to hermeneutics.

THE TEXT AND ITS WORLDS

Contemporary hermeneutical theory approaches a text as a multi-dimensional reality. It sees a text as being written by someone, and coming out of a particular historical situation. It sees a text as being read or heard by someone: texts have audience dimensions. Furthermore, a text has its own character: it might be poetry or a story – this 'genre' is another dimension of the text. Contemporary interpretation theory speaks of these dimensions of the text as the 'worlds' of the text. It holds that there are three such worlds: it terms them 'the world behind the text', 'the world of the text' and 'the world before the text'.

---

3. Part of the background has been the concern, identified in the Enlightenment, that texts were not neutral. As Judith Lieu notes, 'The development of the historical-critical method which has dominated the scholarship of much of the twentieth century was to a large extent the wresting of the Bible out of the grip of the controls of church doctrine, tradition, or other needs.' J. M. Lieu, 'The New Testament and Early Christian Identity' in *Neither Jew nor Greek?*, 2002, London, T&T Clark / Continuum, pp. 191-209, here 201. The issue of the role of theology in the university is not just an academic question. Take, for example, the situations where theological research is not allowed at publicly-funded universities or where theology is not deemed an acceptable form of academic discourse.

It might be noted that the text is an organic whole and none of these dimensions can exist without the others.

It is also possible to look at the worlds of the text as a number of contexts. Consequently, the 'world behind the text' looks at the text through the lens of its historical context; the 'world of the text' looks at the text through the lens of its literary context, and the 'world before the text' looks at the text through the lens of its audience. Presenting each of the worlds permits us not only to have a sense of a particular dimension of the text, but also the interpretative methods associated with it and the challenges each 'world' presents for the academy.

FROM THE 'WORLD BEHIND THE TEXT'
TOWARDS THE 'WORLD BEFORE THE TEXT'

Firstly we may look at the world behind the text. This is the world out of which the text comes. Being concerned with the world behind the text means being 'concerned with what gave rise to the text.'[4] It means being concerned, not only with the history, culture and language of an ancient or sacred author, but also seeking to discover, 'to some extent, the author(s) and her or his historical, theological, and ideological agenda as well as the community to which the text was originally addressed.'[5] Exploring the world behind the text means exploring the world out of which the text came. It means underlining the difference, the distance between the text and the present reader. Concern with the world behind the text can be seen in *Dei Verbum*, the Vatican II Constitution on Divine Revelation where it states,

> Seeing that, in Sacred Scripture, God speaks through humans in human fashion, it follows that the interpreter of Sacred Scripture, in order to ascertain what God wanted to communicate to us, should carefully investigate what meaning the sacred writers really intended, and what God wanted to manifest by means of their words … Rightly to understand what the sacred author wanted to affirm in his work, due attention must be paid both to the customary and characteristic patterns of perception, speech and narrative which prevailed at the

4. Schneiders, *Revelatory Text*, p. 127.
5. Ibid., p. 113.

age of the sacred writer, and to the conventions which the people of his time followed in their dealings with one another.[6]

This is a clear invitation for 'the interpreter of Sacred Scripture' to explore the world behind the text. Its presence in *Dei Verbum*, reinforces a similar invitation in the 1943 Encyclical of Pius XII, *Divino Afflante Spiritu*, and reflects a point of arrival in a long debate about the role of historical research in Roman Catholic exegesis.[7] In so doing, it positions itself in the mainstream of late nineteenth- and mid-twentieth-century research, while bearing witness to what is set forth in its opening paragraphs: 'the invisible God out of the abundance of his love speaks to people as friends and lives among them, so that he may invite and take them into fellowship with himself.'[8] In some ways, in *Divino Afflante Spiritu* and *Dei Verbum*, the Catholic Church caught up with Western academic exegesis, having come to a sense that the interpretation of Scripture had nothing to fear from historical criticism.

However, historical criticism is not the whole story, and the question remains whether this has anything to do with *lectio divina*. As the twentieth century progresses, the investigation of the 'world behind the text' leads to the re-discovery of the audience: first, the ancient audience and then, much later, the contemporary audience.

Early twentieth century criticism had come to realize that what was in the Gospels was not just the writing of anything and everything, but that there was a particular choice involved. This was not new as John the evangelist points out:

> Now Jesus did many other signs in the presence of the disciples, which are not written in this book; but these are written that you may believe that Jesus is the Christ, the Son of God, and that believing you may have life in his name. (Jn 20:30-31)

In the 1920s New Testament critics began to consider *Sitze im Leben* – settings in the life of the early Christian communities – hypothetical

6. Vatican II, Dogmatic Constitution on Divine Revelation, *Dei Verbum*, n. 12.
7. For a profound insight into the parameters and dynamics of these developments, see Pio Laghi, Maurice Gilbert and Albert Vanhoye, *Chiesa e Sacra Scrittura. Un secolo di magistero ecclesiastico e studi biblici* (SubBi 17), 1994, Rome, Editrice PIB.
8. *Dei Verbum*, n. 2

reconstructions of typical community contexts in which a saying or story would have found a resonance and so been used, and which would have been central to its being handed on and consequently finding its way into the Scriptures. Many of these critics were convinced that by careful form analysis one could move back from how a saying or story was used in the early church to how it would have been used in the ministry of Jesus.[9]

One of the effects of Form Criticism was to divide the Gospels into two types of material: the primary material – the sayings of Jesus – and all the rest, secondary material. Form critics in effect saw the Gospels as a necklace of pearls – the sayings of Jesus – joined together by relatively unimportant (and late) secondary material. It is important to note that a shadow of this approach still pertains in the common approach to what is important in the Gospels; many Gospel readers operate out of a two-tier approach – once something is perceived not to have come from the historical Jesus, then it is 'only' from the evangelist.

However, New Testament critics began to realize that the Gospels were more than collections of pearls. The late 1940s saw a shift in focus to those elements in the Gospels that source and form criticism had regarded as secondary: the parts that linked, shaped and ordered traditional material. Critics began to look at the role of the evangelists in shaping what they had received, and began to speak of the editorial activity of the evangelists. This way of looking at the New Testament was called Redaction Criticism. It is the history and critique of an evangelist's editing (in German, *Redaktion*). Each successive evangelist edited or shaped the Gospel material he had received. In 1948, in his 'brilliant short study, '*Die Sturmstillung im Matthäusevangelium,*'... [Günther] Bornkamm concluded that Matthew was not merely handing on the Markan story but was expounding its theological significance in his own way.'[10] Matthew was seen

9. The roots of New Testament form criticism (in German *Formgeschichte*, literally a history of forms) lie in Hermann Gunkel's study of the Psalms. Gunkel's Old Testament insights came into mainstream New Testament research through the influence of Martin Dibelius's *Formgeschichte des Evangeliums* (1919). However, it is Rudolf Bultmann's *Die Geschichte der Synoptischen Tradition* [History of the Synoptic Tradition] (1921; English translation, 1963, Oxford, Blackwell) that was most influential in the twentieth century.

10. Graham N. Stanton, *A Gospel for a New People*, 1992, Edinburgh, T & T Clark, p. 24

not only [as] a hander-on of the Markan narrative, but also its oldest exegete, and in fact the first to interpret the journey of the disciples with Jesus in the storm and the stilling of the storm with reference to discipleship, and that means with reference to the little ship of the Church.[11]

In one sense all of this is still the 'world behind the text', but at the same time the needs of the ancient audience increasingly affected the construction of that world.

'THE WORLD OF THE TEXT'

The emphasis on redaction prepared the way for the major development in New Testament criticism in the latter part of the twentieth century: the arrival of literary and narrative criticism – the realization that, while the evangelist had his theological goals, he achieved them in the way he told his story. The four canonical gospels are narratives; they are essentially stories. Since they are stories, and not systematic treatises, they function as stories: they have a storyline or a plot, they are peopled with characters – heroes and villains – they have beginnings, middles and endings, they surprise us, they console us, they bring us hope, they raise up our hearts.

The 1970s saw a major shift – especially among American and French scholars – in the focus of research. Taking on board insights from post-war literary criticism especially, critics of both Testaments began to explore what was going on in texts as they were. They wondered about what the sacred authors sought to communicate by means of plot and characterization, by means of allusion to other biblical books, or by the choice of words and phrases.[12] Criticism gained a new focus: it

11. Ibid., p. 27.
12. Examples proliferate but two very different studies serve to illustrate both the shift and its potential. For readers of the Hebrew Bible, Robert Alter's *The Art of Biblical Narrative* (1981, New York, Basic Books) made accessible to a more general audience the fruits of the literary-critical reading of the Bible over the previous two decades. In New Testament studies, Alan Culpepper's *The Anatomy of the Fourth Gospel: A Study in Literary Design* (1983, Philadelphia, Fortress) signalled a new perspective in the study of the Gospel of John. In underlining the leadership of this shift among US and French critics, it is to be noted that neither book has yet been translated into German. This is significant in the light of the fact that Martin Buber and Franz Rosenzweig laid firm foundations for the foundations of such a movement in their translation of the Bible.

grew more concerned about texts as they were, and far less about how they came to be.[13] Criticism became concerned about the 'world *of* the text'. The 'world of the text' is the text as language: 'the biblical text, as text, is first and foremost language.'[14] Sandra Schneiders brings to the fore the importance of the world of the text:

> The linguistic nature of scripture as text is so obvious that it has been generally overlooked, or looked through, as scholars have attempted to understand the historical data and the theological meaning of the text … [The biblical text] is even more pervasively linguistic than historical, although its historical character has captivated scholarly attention for centuries.[15]

This has an important resonance with *lectio divina*, insofar as attention to the actual wording is the starting-point – what does the text actually say?

DISCOVERING THE 'WORLD BEFORE THE TEXT'

Biblical texts, as we have noted, are not just ends in themselves. They were written for purposes and, as was seen at the beginning of this paper, they have effects. The text has the power to invite the reader into a possible alternative reality. In effect, the text can create new states of being for its readers and hearers. So we turn to the 'world before, or in front of, the text' – the world of the (post-)modern audience.

In brief, biblical texts, like all texts, have audiences. And also, like all texts, they – to some extent seek to influence those audiences. The awareness that a text – be it written or spoken – can influence a person is something that everyone knows. We learn the persuasive power of speech from earliest childhood. Every parent knows how 'persuasive'

13. This shift in criticism brought with it a shift in critical method. Critics who had been concerned about how texts developed used diachronic methods: they sought to follow the texts through time. Critics who were concerned about texts in their final form were used synchronic methods.

14. Schneiders, *Revelatory Text*, p. 138. While Schneiders and others will point out that the emergence of interest in the text as text is 'due to the so-called turn to language epitomised by Martin Heidegger and his successors in the field of hermeneutical philosophy and Ludwig Wittgenstein and his successors in the field of linguistic philosophy' (*Revelatory Text*, p. 132), it needs to be emphasized that part of the 'success' of the 'world of the text' is due to ability to offer a coherent (or meaningful) interpretation of the text.

15. Ibid.

a child can be. Since ancient times cultures have explored how texts affect their audiences. In the fourth century BCE, Aristotle could define rhetoric 'as the faculty of discovering the possible means of persuasion in reference to any subject whatever.'[16] Furthermore, he realized that the function of rhetoric ...

> is to deal with things about which we deliberate, but for which we have no systematic rules; and in the presence of such hearers as are unable to take a general view of many stages, or to follow a lengthy sequence of argument.[17]

As well as dealing with that which overtly seeks to persuade (e.g., exhortations, speeches, letters), Aristotle came to understand that 'each class of things' has its rhetoric or persuasive power.[18] Thus, even on the basis of Aristotelian rhetoric, it is possible to speak of a rhetoric of drama and a rhetoric of fiction.[19] It is possible to discover the rhetoric of any discourse, including liturgy or worship. In the Liturgy, not only does the believer celebrate her or his salvation and worship the Lord, the Liturgy also seeks to move the believer or the unbeliever.

This is an indicator of the 'world *before* the text'. The 'world before the text' is the result of the capacity of the text to 'create a world into which the reader is invited.'[20] You may remember the response of 'Julia' at the beginning of this paper: she 'hated having to say, 'Crucify him! Crucify him!'" The Gospel narrative of the Passion created a world into which she was 'invited' and which she found herself entering. We see the story becoming 'the vehicle that carries the reader into a possible alternative reality.'[21]

One of the notable characteristics of scholarship in the last 30

16. *Rhetoric,* I.ii.1 (Loeb Classical Library, p. 15)

17. Ibid., I.iii.12 (Loeb Classical Library, p. 23).

18. Ibid., I.ii.22 (Loeb Classical Library, p. 33). Aristotle can maintain, 'I mean by dialectical and rhetorical syllogisms those which are concerned with what we call 'topics' which may be applied alike to Law, Physics, Politics and many other sciences that differ in kind ...' Ibid., I.ii.21 (Loeb Classical Library, p. 31).

19. See, for example, Wayne C. Booth, *The Rhetoric of Fiction* (second ed., 1983, Chicago, University of Chicago Press). The first edition of Booth's work dates from 1961, bearing witness to the dynamism of literary criticism in the years after the Second World War.

20. Schneiders, *The Revelatory Text,* p. 167.

21. Ibid.

years has been the rediscovery of biblical rhetoric and the deeper significance of the text's power to persuade. It proponents would call it the New Rhetoric and maintain that,

> [t]he essence of rhetoric, like that of poetry, is not communication but the creation of new states of being... The power of persuasion alludes to the mystery of meaning that comes through language.[22]

The 'world before the text' is the world of the audience. There are critics, such as Stanley Fish, who would place even greater emphasis on the audience dimension and maintain that 'the reader's activities are at the center of attention, where they are not regarded as leading to meaning but as having meaning.'[23] Returning to Julia, we begin to appreciate why critics such as Fish can maintain this.

PHILOSOPHICAL ROOTS

The hermeneutics and reading strategies of Schneiders, Wuellner and Fish are very different but they have their roots in the same place, namely that encountering a text changes a person. In philosophical terms, the reflections of critics such as Schneiders and Wuellner find their home in the philosophy of Martin Heidegger. Heidegger (1889-1976) was concerned with the question of being. In seeking to answer the question, 'what is being?', he first seeks to describe the structure of human existence. For him, human existence is essentially relational, that is, the mode of being of the human person is being in the world. This being-in-the-world, which he terms *Dasein* (literally, there-being/being there), constitutes the being of humans. It may be presented as follows:

22. The Bible and Culture Collective, *The Postmodern Bible* (1995, New Haven CT, Yale University Press), p. 170. The collaborative character of the volume notwithstanding, the chapter on rhetorical criticism (pp. 149–186) is clearly the work of Wilhelm Wuellner. The influence of Gadamer's hermeneutics on Wuellner is palpable: even the casual reader will not fail to notice the citation from Gadamer in the article's epigraph. However, the depth of Wuellner's conversation with Gadamer is evident in his *Hermeneutics and Rhetorics. From 'Truth and Method' to 'Truth and Power'* (1989, Stellenbosch: Center for Hermeneutical Studies).

23. In David Lodge with Nigel Woods (eds.), *Modern Criticism and Theory: A Reader* (second ed., 2000, Harlow: Longman), p. 296. This is in opposition to what Fish would term a reading of the text which is 'positivist, holistic, and spatial' (ibid.) where there is one meaning ('a sense') (ibid., p. 295) and where that meaning 'is embedded or encoded in the text, and that it can be taken in at a single glance.' (ibid., p. 297)

This manner of existence is not merely accidental, it is a necessity of thought in the sense that the world as I find it is constitutive of my existence, not merely the place in which I have my existence. There is no separation possible. My preoccupations in the world, my tasks, concerns, cares, pursuits, exemplify the manner of my existence: I can free myself from this or that task or care, but never from preoccupation of some sort. My immediate world (the world immediately present to me) is the world of my concerns, not the world of objects immediately present.[24]

Two remarks are in order. *Dasein* is characterized by its potential: finding myself in the world opens up the possibility of responding to it, and because – until death – I will always be in the world, this responding is never accomplished. '*Dasein*, then, being a possibility, exists by projecting itself … [and] the meaning of human existence is [worked out] in the possibilities of action of *Dasein*. I give sense to what is about me by making use of it.'[25]

The encounter with a text changes my *Dasein*. According to Heidegger, the essence of language lies in its 'ability to evoke the nature of things, but in such a way that the painful difference between thing and world becomes manifest.'[26] He continues, 'Language speaks. The human being speaks insofar as she or he corresponds to language. Listening is the corresponding.'[27]

Here again a bridge to *lectio divina* can be discerned. Reading lies

24. H. J. Blackham, *Six Existentialist Thinkers* (1951, London, Routledge & Kegan Paul; reprint 1961), pp. 88-89.

25. Ibid., p. 92. Here too we see Paul Ricoeur's roots in Heidegger: 'The sense of a text is not behind the text, but in front of it. It is not something hidden but something disclosed. What has to be understood is not the initial situation of discourse, *but what points towards a possible world* … [my emphasis]. Understanding has less than ever to do with the author and his situation. It seeks to grasp the world-propositions opened up by the reference of the text.' (*Interpretation Theory: Discourse and the Surplus of Meaning,* 1976, Fort Worth, TX, Texas Christian University Press, p. 87). The present discussion seeks to set forth a principal line of argument in the light of Heidegger's hermeneutics and therefore, in the interests of clarity, does not engage with the question of authentic and inauthentic modes of existence.

26. Martin Heidegger, *Unterwegs zur Sprache* (fourth ed.; Pfullingen: Neske, 1971), 26ff; cited after Werner Jeanrond, *Theological Hermeneutics: Development and Significance* (London: SCM, 1994), p. 63.

27. Ibid.,p. 33. The order of Jeanrond's translation which ends, 'the corresponding is listening' has been transposed in the interests of clarity.

at the heart of *lectio divina*; when we read, a new set of possibilities is created, a new world is projected and our *Dasein* changes. Reading is ultimately a threshold; beyond that threshold is listening. Without listening, without silence, little of God's word can be heard.[28] In *lectio divina*, the word comes to awaken the heart and 'evok[es] the nature of things ... in such a way that the painful difference between thing and world becomes manifest.' *Lectio divina*, as a way of reading, brings the reader of the sacred text to 'discern ... "the world before the text" ... [so that] the ultimate goal of interpretation, the existential augmentation of the reader, takes place in her or his participation, through the text, in the world before the text.'[29]

If, as I have just argued, a change in one's being – transformation – is the ultimate goal of the reading that is *lectio divina*, the 'world before the text' becomes key. Is then the pressing challenge for the academy to move more and more into the 'world before the text'? Put another way, how must the academy meet Julia?

THE CHALLENGE FOR THE ACADEMY

Lectio Divina is a walk toward God, and for that reason, as in any walk, so in this, everything has to be proportioned to the pace, the strength, the rhythm of those who are walking.[30]

Reading for transformation is at the heart of *lectio divina*. How do we read for transformation? We focus on our reading! The way to the 'world before the text' is through the 'world of the text'. This is the key challenge for the academy at the present time. Suggesting that the 'world before the text' is the privileged access point may meet with little explicit opposition, but a quick glance at university biblical programmes and introductory textbooks tells another story. Biblical programmes at university – and the second level syllabi that mirror

28. It might be noted that without a seeking of silence, there can be no listening. Furthermore, without silence – which essentially is existential space – there can be no action. Without silence, we do not act in new ways. Without silence, the academic does not come to a new understanding; without silence, the human being does not authentically change. Without silence, there is no enduring repentance.

29. Schneiders, *Revelatory Text*, p. 167.

30. Mario Masini, *Lectio Divina: An Ancient Prayer That Is Ever New*, 1998, New York, Alba House, pp. 99-100.

them – generally begin with significant introduction into the historical and cultural background of the Bible. In other words, biblical education generally begins with the 'world behind the text'.[31]

The profound coherence of *lectio divina* – an ancient way – with contemporary biblical hermeneutics points to the relative barrenness of such a gateway into the Scriptures today and calls for another approach. It needs to be emphasized that the 'world behind the text' is an absolutely essential dimension of a balanced interpretation of the Scriptures, but it is a very barren point of entry.

The barrenness is due to many factors. The key factor, which escapes most commentators because they themselves do not suffer from it, is that many of those who are being introduced to the Bible have never read or heard the Scriptures.[32] This is not the case for many senior academics who, for cultural or religious reasons, have a broad and deep familiarity with the Bible. However, for many who enter the academy, all familiarity is lacking. The academy esteems experts and expertise. After all, such is part of its *raison d'être.* However it is easy to drift into a

> [h]istorical Positivism [which] regards the philologist or expert historian as the most appropriate audience for the text, for the philologist is 'the true reader for whom the text is written, one who, as a 'super-reader,' can better understand the author's use of sources than the author himself did. It is only the philologist who, within the later horizon of a more complete, if not actually universal, knowledge, is able to recognize sources upon which an author has drawn, whether consciously or unconsciously.[33]

'Super-reading' is one of the more reliable ways of suffocating the living word. Overcoming it brings us to the next challenge: to realize

31. This was also the case in many 'pastoral' programmes where what was offered was almost exclusively from the world behind the text.

32. Qumran scholar, James A. Sanders raised this matter at a public lecture in the University of Fribourg in November 1989. He remarked that when he returned to teach Bible in California in the late 1950s or early 1960s, he became very aware that he was speaking of biblical texts in a vacuum: his students, unlike his peers, had no real knowledge of the biblical text. It is worth noting that he was not teaching in a Roman Catholic seminary and that is almost fifty years ago.

33. Francis Schüssler Fiorenza, 'The Crisis of Scriptural Authority: Interpretation and Reception' Int 44 (1990), 365 and citing Hans Robert Jauss, *Question and Answer: Forms of Dialogic Understanding,* 1989, Minneapolis MI, University of Minnesota Press, p. 219.

that, while the historical is foundational, it is precisely that: the foundation. It is not the best entrance. A person does not enter her or his home by digging up the foundations of the house! We enter through a doorway.

The relationship between foundation and doorway has been well expressed by John Darr:

> The historical critical methods were well-designed for their specific tasks, and they have greatly increased our understanding of earliest Christianity. However, our fixation with them has, to a great extent, blinded us to the insight that each New Testament narrative evokes for its audience a unique narrative world – an ordered whole in which elements mutually condition and illuminate one another – to be studied on its own terms.[34]

This is clearly not to argue for the abandonment of a historical critique of the biblical text and its associated diachronic methods.[35] Nor is it to imply a wielding of the words of Pope Leo IX in *Providentissimus Deus*, his biblical encyclical of 1893, that historical research can only 'gnaw the bark of the Sacred Scripture, and never attain its pith.'[36] Indeed, without a historical optic, contemporary readers of the Bible risk never tasting the 'otherness' of the Bible – in both Testaments – and being condemned to the interpretative shallows. To keep the historical in play is a key task of the academy.[37] Otherwise, we cannot hear the Bible with its own voice. However, the way in which the academy keeps the historical in play lies at the heart of this challenge.

The core challenge to the Academy that comes from *lectio divina* is, I suggest, to enter by the broad door of the narrative.

---

34. John A. Darr, *On Character Building: The Reader and the Rhetoric of Characterization in Luke-Acts*, 1992, Louisville KY, Westminster John Knox, p. 12.

35. John Barton's acute observation that '[t]here has been and is plenty of interest in history that is not at all driven by a critical mind-set' is worthy of note in this context. (John Barton, *The Nature of Biblical Criticism*, 2007, Louisville KY, Westminster John Knox Press, p. 68.

36. *Providentissimus Deus*, n. 15.

37. For a stimulating exploration of the essential nature of a historical optic see John J. Collins, 'Historical Criticism in the Postmodern Age', *PIBA* 28 (2005), pp. 28-47. A more developed exploration can be found in Barton's *Nature of Biblical Criticism* (see note 35 above).

THE WORLD OF THE TEXT: THE BEST ENTRY POINT
– A CORE VALUE IN *LECTIO DIVINA*

Why is this the best entry point? Because it first pays attention to what is written, and only secondarily encourages the reader to seek explanations for what is not immediately clear, given the 'otherness' of the text. Ultimately it permits us to engage with the message of the text more directly.

Ideally this is where both *lectio divina* and scholarly reading begins – paying attention. The role of the historical and critical 'background' material then becomes important in preventing the reader from jumping to conclusions or misconceiving what the text says through lack of appreciation of significant differences between ancient and modern life-experience, culture, social conventions, and so on. But *lectio divina* also challenges the academic reader to submit to the text rather than sitting in judgment upon it – to become a 'servant-reader' rather than a 'super-reader'. For attention to the biblical text soon reveals that these texts are meant to evoke a response. The reader is meant to be engaged and transformed by the text.

In literary criticism, reader response theory has also suggested that each time a text is read, it will be read and responded to differently. Frances Young has made a similar observation concerning Augustine: 'Augustine had previously read Paul but … he had read Paul in another way.'[38] Augustine is reading Paul. He is reading Paul for himself and, as he grew older, his reading of Paul changed! Young continues:

> The function of scholarly discussion and debate is surely to sharpen our awareness, not to settle questions which are ultimately unsettleable… [W]e should not underestimate the difference that exegetical engagement made [for Augustine]. One knows the experience of accepting traditions of interpretation *until one engages specifically with the text for oneself* (italics mine). Then things emerge from the text that one has not imagined before, though one may have read it many times.[39]

Contemporary universities are places where 'interdisciplinarity'

38. Frances Young, *Biblical Exegesis and the Formation of Christian Culture,* 1997, Cambridge, Cambridge University Press, p. 267.
39. Ibid., p. 269.

is prized – at least in theory! One of the greatest challenges in the academic life and in the spiritual life is to continue to grow, not to stagnate. And that growth occurs by 'putting out into the deep' (Lk 5:4). This is a significant challenge within academic theology: it is not only exegetes and laity who may (or indeed must) read the Scriptures, the theologian must read the Scriptures and learn to read them well. Going from 'super-reader' to 'servant- reader' within the academy is an enormous challenge. It is in this context of 'sharpening our awareness' that we may read for ourselves that I have indicated a number of challenges from (and for) Scripture in an academic setting.

CONCLUSION

What this means is that we never have the final word on the text; we always remain in dialogue. Yet history is essential because it keeps us grounded in the *Dasein* of the other. So it is vital that Julia and the academic read together, but in such a way that the academic learns to kneel and wash feet, and Julia is not dis-empowered.

> … my preference is to work with the text of Scripture itself. For I take it that one element in the renewal of interaction between Scripture and theology is to show how theological thinking can be enhanced by attention to scriptural exegesis and interpretation; and if that is so, then it is more fruitful not just to talk about it but to try to do it.[40]

The core value of *lectio divina* is that it gives us the text, so that the biblical text is what we have at the beginning and what we have at the end. The 'world behind the text' is a construct, though often an illuminating one. The 'world before or in front of the text' is the potential of the text to transform us. The 'world of the text' is, as it were, 'tangible' – a kind of sacrament whereby we receive the very presence of God's Word. It is the table from which we receive the very bread of life.[41]

---

40. Walter Moberly, 'Jonah, God's Objectionable Mercy, and the Way of Wisdom,' in David F. Ford and Graham Stanton, eds., *Reading Texts, Seeking Wisdom. Scripture and Theology*, 2003, London, SCM Press, p. 155.

41. See *Dei Verbum*, n. 21.

Combining *Lectio Divina* and
Historical Critical Method

The Challenge in Parish and Pastoral Settings

CHRIS HAYDEN

DEI VERBUM, the Constitution of the Second Vatican Council on Divine Revelation, tells us: 'access to sacred Scripture ought to be open wide to the Christian faithful.' (n. 22). The document goes on to say: 'The sacred Synod forcefully and specifically exhorts all the Christian faithful … to learn "the surpassing knowledge of Jesus Christ" (Phil 3:8) by frequent reading of the divine Scriptures.' To these exhortations is added the well-known caution of St Jerome: 'Ignorance of the Scriptures is ignorance of Christ.'

In the same document, there are two further statements that, taken together, chart a course for any attempt to combine *lectio divina* with historical critical method. *Dei Verbum* insists that 'the books of Scripture, firmly, faithfully and without error, teach that truth which God, for the sake of our salvation, wished to see confided to the sacred Scripture.' (n. 11) It is that conviction that led the Council to urge all the baptized to pray the Scriptures, that is, to do *lectio divina*.

There is a further statement that is, in a sense, in tension with that first conviction. *Dei Verbum* also tells us: 'the words of God, expressed in the words of men, are in every way like human language, just as the Word of the eternal Father, when he took on himself the flesh of human weakness, became like men.' (n. 13) Here, the Council acknowledges that Scripture can be prey to all the complexities and conditionings of any other written word, and there is a need to work through those

Chris Hayden, former Scripture teacher at St Peter's Seminary, Wexford, and St John's Seminary, Waterford, has published *A Practical Guide to Lectio Divina* (2001)

complexities and conditionings with care.

Clearly, then, the Second Vatican Council mandates not just reading, but critically informed reading of the Bible. The Church wants people to pray the Scriptures; it wants those who do *lectio divina* to benefit from sound biblical scholarship, and it wants sound scholarship to support those who do *lectio divina*.

Many believers – perhaps a growing number – want to read their Bibles and find nourishment there for their discipleship. But when they open the Bible, they are opening a very diverse collection of writings that begins with one rather arcane literary genre, mythology, and ends with another, equally arcane one, apocalyptic. In between there is a fair share of complexity. How do we help those who wish to pray to Scriptures to navigate their encounter with the word of God; a word which has taken on all the weakness of human language?

This is precisely the pastoral challenge involved in combining *lectio divina* with historical critical method.[1] It's not a question of assimilating spirituality to scholarship, or of attempting to make mini-exegetes of people who are in fact thirsting for an encounter with Christ in Scripture. Nor is it about cherry-picking scholarship for nuggets that seem appropriate to the spiritual journey. The challenge is to keep before us the fact that the Scriptures which are our word of life can also be 'hard to understand' (2 Pet 3:16). Neither spiritual fervour alone, nor technical expertise alone, can draw out the full richness of the Scriptures as *both* the truth given to us for our salvation, *and* the word of God in human language. There is, therefore, a serious pastoral challenge to establish a partnership between *lectio divina* and historical critical method.

THE RELATIONSHIP BETWEEN *LECTIO DIVINA* AND CRITICAL SCHOLARSHIP

In my own experience of introducing people to the Scriptures at a parish/pastoral level, I have found a number of approaches particularly helpful, and I propose to share some of them. But before doing that, I'd like to dwell a little on some broader issues concerning biblical

1. In this paper, I use the term 'historical critical method' as shorthand for all critical approaches to the Bible, whether or not their primary methodology is historical.

scholarship and the fortunes of biblical ministry at parish level.

First, a cautionary tale. I once heard a parish priest, a learned man, who, on the feast of the Epiphany, began his homily with the words: 'Biblical scholarship now assures us that there were, in fact, no wise men.' In one fell swoop, that preacher managed to trample on the imagination of his congregation, to make impostors of three of the figures in the crib at his side, and to divorce his scholarly reading from the faith life of his flock. It's the last of those three achievements that I want to consider here.

When biblical scholarship and the life of faith are divorced from each other, there can be two opposite, but equally negative, effects. On the one hand, the life of faith can retreat from the sane, critical, rational grounding provided by sound scholarship, and fall into fundamentalism, which is at heart indifference to critical reading. Fundamentalism needs to be considered a significant pastoral concern, and helping enthusiastic readers of the Bible to guard against it is a basic duty of pastoral care. On the other hand, divorced from the life of faith, academic approaches to Scripture can begin to look like, or can actually become, ivory tower exercises in irrelevance. I would suggest that the marriage between *lectio divina* and critical biblical scholarship be considered an indissoluble one.

But to explore the question a little further: is there scope for a pastoral approach to the Bible which keeps biblical scholarship at arm's length? Would it be wise, pastorally, to seek to return to an allegedly 'pre-critical' approach to the Bible? In point of fact, critical reading of the Bible is not a recent development, and we would have to go back a very long way indeed in order to arrive at a pre-critical time. To be truly *pre*-critical, we would, for example, have to go further back than Origen (died 253), who, even though he tends to be associated with uncritical (or a-critical) allegorizing, was in fact committed to critical reading.[2] Origen was a serious textual critic; he challenged traditional convictions regarding authorship of individual biblical books; he didn't shrink from the differences between the Synoptic Gospels.

I mention Origen not out of any particular historical interest, but

2. On Origen as a critical reader of the Bible, cf. chapter 3 of Johnson and Kurz, *The Future of Catholic Biblical Scholarship*, 2002, Grand Rapids, MN, Eerdmans.

to make the pastorally relevant point that critical reading of the Bible is not a recent invention. When the impatient, thirsting people in our Bible classes or *lectio divina* groups question the relevance, or even the reverence, of a critical approach to the Bible, we might do well to let them know that, in addition to being mandated by the Church, this kind of approach has a long and worthy pedigree. It was, for example, Origen, and not some post-conciliar upstart scholar, who once observed of the creation accounts in Genesis:

> I do not think anyone will doubt that these are figurative expressions which indicate certain mysteries through a semblance of history and not through actual event.[3]

Critical study is extremely important – so important that those who engage in biblical ministry at parish or pastoral level need to take care to be properly informed by the best available scholarship. But *lectio divina* is not simply the breaking down of scholarly insights.

I think it is helpful to view *lectio divina* and critical scholarship as polar opposites. What is scholarship? It is an attempt to *master the word*. What is *lectio divina*? It is an attempt to be *mastered by the word*. If the biblical scholar seeks to *grasp* the word, then the practitioner of *lectio divina* seeks to be *grasped by* that same word. It follows that biblical scholarship should precede, rather than preclude, biblical spirituality. The challenge to those who seek to provide a bridge between scholarship and *lectio divina* is, in the pastoral context, to present and apply scholarship as a prelude to a lived spirituality.

FOUR KEYS FOR A CRITICALLY INFORMED
PASTORAL PRESENTATION OF *LECTIO DIVINA*

How can those who have sought to *understand* the word, help those who wish to *stand under* the word? I would like to outline four approaches that in my experience have helped those who wish to experience the Bible as the living and effective word. They are approaches that can give people an initial, broad appreciation of the Scriptures. I have found them useful as an introduction to the Bible

---

3. Quoted in Steinmetz, 'The Superiority of Pre-Critical Exegesis.' *Theology Today* 37 (1980), pp. 27-38.

for those interested in making the Scriptures an integral part of their Christian discipleship.

Learning to think biblically

First, *lectio divina* is, in large part, about learning to think biblically – having our outlook formed by the contours of Scripture at their very broadest. In order to think biblically, one needs to learn those contours, and at a pastoral level, I have found it very useful to present the overall narrative framework of the Bible. At its simplest, that narrative framework can be described as consisting of four parts (in effect, a play in four acts, with a couple of those acts having many individual scenes).

The four parts are creation, fall, redemption and fulfilment. I would suggest that everything from Genesis chapter 1 to Revelation chapter 22 can be related to that broad schema. Obviously not every page of the Bible is narrative or ostensibly historical, but even the largest non-historical section of the Bible, the wisdom writings, can be presented as the efforts of believers to be faithful to God in their particular situations; situations which are always marked by the tension between the fall and its effects, on the one hand, and the redeeming work of God, on the other.

Those of us who have some theological and biblical study under our belts need to be aware of excessive familiarity. Those four simple terms – creation, fall, redemption and fulfilment – carry an entire world-view: the biblical world-view. They tell us that in the biblical understanding, creation is good and the human person is the high point of that creation: created, willed, loved by God. They tell us that the grace of creation is unravelled by the *dis*grace of the fall, which in essence is disobedience, forgetfulness of God. They reassure us that that the fall is not the last word, but that, in parallel (and in tension) with the history of sin, there is a history of grace, the history of redemption. And the last of those four terms, fulfilment, promises us that despite the fall and its consequences, God's purpose of redemption will prevail, leading to the fulfilment of his designs.

In practice, I tend to present creation and fulfilment, the first and last of those four 'acts,' as specific moments. Creation occurred at a moment in the past, and fulfilment will occur at a moment in the future. Between those times, the believer lives with the effects of the fall and the effects of God's work of redemption.

A question that this perspective can bring to *lectio divina* is: 'How does this biblical text (book, passage, etc.) address this particular moment in my ongoing experience of both sin and grace, of both fall and redemption?' Or: 'How does this biblical text relate to my present experience of discipleship?'

When the broad, four-part narrative has been grasped, then both the particular text and the particular experience of discipleship can be related to it, and when such connections are made, they provide an impetus for *lectio divina*.

The Whole and the Parts

A second key I have found useful for *lectio divina* at a pastoral level is the insistence that the whole is greater than the sum of the parts. This has an obvious connection to the idea of an over-arching biblical narrative, but it relates more specifically to individual books of the Bible. A lectionary – or *pericope* – approach to *lectio divina* is very much richer if it is based on an overall understanding of the book within which a given text is located.

This can perhaps be seen most clearly in the case of the Gospels: where a passage taken in isolation might not yield its full fruit. It may speak much more clearly when read with some awareness (however slight) of the guiding concerns of the evangelist in question. Matthew's predilection for Old Testament citations, for example, or Mark's rather downbeat presentation of disciples and discipleship, or Luke's fascination what is happening *today*, or John's interest in Jewish feasts – all of these can be presented as significant pointers towards an overall understanding of each Gospel. Within that overall understanding, specific texts take on greater colour and texture, and those whose *lectio divina* is informed by such richness are more likely to succeed in making connections between word and life, between text and discipleship. We do not have to give every *lectio divina* group a course on the Synoptic problem, or on Johannine theology, but a little input rooted in solid critical scholarship can go a long way.

Three Questions

A third key which I have found helpful in presenting *lectio divina*, and which can help to keep the practice of *lectio divina* open to the insights of critical scholarship, is what one might call the three-questions approach. Traditionally, *lectio divina* is presented as a series of steps or stages: *lectio, meditatio, oratio, contemplatio*; reading, meditation, prayer and contemplation.[4] I will not dwell here on contemplation, the fourth of these stages. Wrestling with this hard-to-define term might take us a little far afield, and in any case, contemplation is probably better considered a 'passivity' than an activity.

But the first three stages – reading, prayer and meditation – can be described, and the relationships between them can brought out, by means of three guiding questions. In *lectio*/reading, one is asking: 'What does the text say in itself? In meditation, one is asking: 'What does the text say to me / to us?' In prayer, the question becomes: 'What does the text lead me / us to say?'

There is a wonderful – and wonderfully simply – logic to those three questions. They help to draw a clear line from reading to reflection to prayer (I have witnessed the occasional 'aha!' moment when the connectedness and wholeness offered by those three questions dawns).

Some observations regarding the three-questions approach are in order. The first question ('what does the text say in itself?') implies that reading / *lectio* is about understanding the meaning of the text. At this stage the contribution of critical scholarship is necessary. Without getting bogged down in questions of hermeneutics or layers of meaning, some degree of critical realism at the beginning of the encounter with the text is essential if the rest of the process of *lectio divina* is to be well grounded.

The contribution of the historical critical method falls under the rubric of 'what does the text say in itself?' Critical scholarship can thus be seen as intrinsic to the process of *lectio divina*, rather than merely a prelude, or a chore to be dispensed with as quickly as possible so that

---

4. The 1993 Pontifical Biblical Commission Document, *The Interpretation of the Bible in the Church*, defines *lectio divina* as: 'A reading, on an individual or communal level, of a more or less lengthy passage of Scripture, received as the Word of God and leading, at the prompting of the Spirit, to meditation, prayer and contemplation.'

the real business of meditation and prayer can be started.

The middle question ('What does the text say to me/us?') covers the stage of meditation or reflection on the biblical text. It is precisely because the text has been properly understood in itself that one is free to apply it realistically to one's own situation. Meditation calls for imagination, but not for fantasy. There is no danger of fantasy taking over when meditation is grounded in a sound appropriation of the meaning of the text.

With regard to the third question ('What does the text lead me/ us to say?'), it is worth emphasising that this question is answered not only with words (which are, of course, important) but with a life that speaks. Here, one might think of the admonition of St Francis to his followers: 'Preach always; use words if necessary.' Pastorally speaking, it is important to stress that *lectio divina* is not some abstract pious practice: it is about entering into God's plan, enfleshing the word. It should not become pietistic or individualistic.

Scripture Received in the Liturgy

A fourth pastoral key to *lectio divina* is the reception of Scripture in the Church's liturgical usage. I refer not to the use of Scriptural texts in the liturgy, but to the many liturgical prayers and reflections which contain syntheses of biblical themes and theology, and which can be used to illustrate the biblical background to the liturgical and sacramental life of the Church. (This can be quite a revelation to Catholics who are used to the notion that theirs is a ritual, or sacramental, rather than a biblical faith.) Here, I present three examples.

First, in the liturgy of baptism, one of the options given for the blessing of water is a prayer (also used during the Easter Vigil) which provides a panorama of biblical narrative and motifs:

Father, you give us grace through sacramental signs, which tell us of the wonders of your unseen power. In baptism we use your gift of water, which you have made a rich symbol of the grace you give us in this sacrament. At the very dawn of creation, your Spirit breathed on the waters, making them the wellspring of all holiness. The waters of the great flood you made a sign of the waters of baptism, that make an end of sin and a new beginning of goodness. Through the waters of the Red Sea you led Israel out of slavery, to be an image of God's holy people, set free from sin by baptism. In the waters of the Jordan your Son was baptised by John and anointed with the Spirit. Your Son willed that water and blood should flow from his side as he hung upon the cross. After his resurrection he told his disciples: 'Go out and teach all nations, baptising them in the name of the Father and of the Son and of the Holy Spirit.' Father, look now with love upon your Church, and unseal for her the fountain of baptism...

A second example, taken from Eucharistic Prayer IV, illustrates the four-fold schema of creation-fall-redemption-fulfilment, and shows the connectedness of the two Testaments:

Father, we acknowledge your greatness: all your actions show your wisdom and love. Your formed us in your own likeness and set us over the whole world to serve you, our creator, and to rule over all creatures [creation]. Even when we disobeyed you and lost your friendship [fall], you did not abandon us to the power of death, but helped all people to seek and find you. Again and again you offered us a covenant, and through the prophets taught us to hope for salvation [redemption]. Father, you so loved the world that in the fullness of time [fulfilment] you sent your only Son to be our Saviour ...[5]

A final example, a passage from St John Chrysostom used in the Office of Readings from the Liturgy of the Hours of Good Friday, links Exodus, Passover and Eucharist:

Do you wish to know of the power of Christ's blood? Let us go back to the ancient accounts of what took place in Egypt, where Christ's blood is foreshadowed. Moses said: 'Sacrifice a lamb without blemish and smear the doors with its blood.' What does this mean? Can the blood of a sheep without reason save man who is endowed with reason? Yes, Moses replies, not because it is blood but because it is a figure of the Lord's blood. So today if the devil sees, not the

---

5. This extract has been altered for inclusiveness.

blood of the figure smeared on the doorsteps, but the blood of the reality smeared on the lips of the faithful, which are the doors of the temple of Christ, with all the more reason will he draw back.

Overall, some insight into how the Bible is received in the Church's liturgy can be very useful in showing that *lectio divina* is in complete continuity with the sacramental life of those who wish to pray the Scriptures.

THE PASTORAL CHALLENGE

With regard to *lectio divina*, the single biggest pastoral challenge is to give people an appetite for the Bible. Serious Bible reading, at least among Catholics, remains something of a minority sport. How do we convey to people that the Bible, the Word of God, offers a wonderfully liberating and hopeful view of the world? How do we put it across that, while it is by no means a reference guide, or a book of ready solutions to life's conundrums, the Bible, in its over-arching narrative and in its motifs and themes, is the living and effective word, *verbum vivens et efficax*?

Part – perhaps a large part – of the answer is to seek to become imbued with a biblical outlook ourselves; to become half-decent advertisements for a biblically grounded discipleship. It's not, thankfully, that we have to be walking saints in order to propagate *lectio divina* with reasonable effectiveness, but if we have a solid personal grasp of the utter relevance of the Bible to our own discipleship, then we are more likely to be able to convey that relevance to others. The words of John Wesley are worth dwelling on: 'If you set yourself on fire, people will come along to watch you burn.'

As the two disciples on the road to Emmaus pointed out, where the Scriptures are opened, hearts will burn. Critical scholarship may, at times, have appeared to close rather than to open the Bible, but that need not be so. Its best insights, themselves critically appropriated, can help in the pastoral task of opening the Scriptures through *lectio divina*.

Lectio Divina in Trinidad
According to the Method of
Fr Michel de Verteuil

PAT ELIE

I T IS 7.00 pm on a Thursday evening in Santa Rosa, Arima, and people are gathering in the parish hall for their weekly *lectio divina* meeting as they have been doing for the last twelve years. The size of the group has varied but there is a core group of between eight and ten people, including a young on-the-job-trainee, two housewives, a care-giver at a home for the physically and mentally handicapped, a carpenter, an NGO worker, a secretary and a civil servant. Their education level varies, some have had little formal education, two are university graduates. But these differences matter little to the group. Over the years they have come to know at a very deep level that each person is equal before the text. Each person has the confidence that comes from knowing that their story is unique and true and sacred because it is part of the sacred history that is the Scripture.

After an opening prayer and song, the group reads aloud together the Gospel text of the coming Sunday. For the members of the group, the text is sacred, it is the Word of God, it is a place where they meet God. So reading the text is a holy moment. After a short silence, the group facilitator gives an introduction to the text, commenting on whether it is Ordinary Time or one of the seasons of the year, *e.g.*, Advent or Lent, each with its own focus and flavour. The facilitator also puts the text in the broader context of Jesus' story, *e.g.*, his being on his

Pat Elie is a facilitator of Applied Scripture (*lectio divina*) in Trinidad, West Indies. She worked for years with Fr Michel de Verteuil, a leading exponent of *lectio divina.*

In preparing this paper, she drew on the experiences of many *lectio* practitioners in Trinidad, including the *lectio divina* priests study group led by Fr Michel de Verteuil as well as the *lectio divina* Bible Class of Santa Rosa Parish, Arima. Heartfelt gratitude to all for their input and support.

way to Jerusalem, and may comment on some of the other characters in the text, *e.g.*, the lepers, Samaritans, the Pharisees. The text is initially teased out to suggest different ways that it may correspond to the life experience of the group. All the members then share their personal reflection, approaching the text from their unique standpoint – as housewife, a single parent, an NGO worker, care-giver, a secretary, etc. Throughout each personal sharing, everyone listens respectfully. If necessary, the facilitator may help someone to recognize their story more fully in the Gospel story. These personal sharings then give way to an open discussion during which the reflection is widened and insights may be explored more fully.

Each person is free to stay with a phrase, a paragraph or the entire text. They share their reflections, using the words of the text, savouring the words and phrases that speak to them, interpreting the metaphors and imagery that engage their story. The reflections move from the personal or intimate to the wider national community, to the world. Members relate the story in the text to the story of their own lives or those close to them, to some happening in Trinidad, in the wider world. The context may be their work, their families, current affairs, the local political scene, something going on in another part of the world. As part of their reflection, members think about who or what was Jesus for them in the specific context of the Gospel text of that Sunday. They share any insight or wisdom that they gained from their reflection. Wisdom is a deep truth, a deep insight into life, that is new and changes our consciousness – the way we see people and issues. It is not a call to action. It is never moralistic but has moral implications.

Each person closes their individual reflections by praying in the words of the Gospel text, prayers of thanksgiving, humility and petition. They always end on a high note: 'What are we celebrating this week?'

The members of the group have been reading aloud and reflecting on the Gospel text on their own since the beginning of the week, thus allowing the Word to interact more fully with their own memories and consciousness. This emphasizes the importance of hearing and listening to the Word spoken. They will continue with the text until the Sunday celebration of the Mass. Each person keeps a journal to record their reflections. The use of the journal helps them to be consistent in their *lectio* reflection. It is also very useful to look back and see where you were three years ago.

The combination of individual reflection and group sharing facilitates the proper practice of *lectio divina*. Personal reflection is essential to allow the Gospel story to engage an individual's story. Being part of and sharing with a group helps to deepen this engagement with the text. Individuals may connect to different sections of the text. The shared reflections of the group give everyone an overall sense of the text, even though they stay with the section of the text that speaks most deeply to them. Listening and discussing the stories and insights shared by group members helps to widen and deepen individual reflection, helps them to gain deeper insights and understanding, helps individuals to come more fully to wisdom. Very importantly, a group helps members to stay with the discipline of the method. The group corrects itself, it helps its members to keep their balance – to avoid moralizing or condemning themselves or others.

WHAT HAPPENS

I now propose to report on how the group reflected on the Gospel text for the Twenty-ninth Sunday of Ordinary Time, Year B:

> Jesus called them to him and said to them, 'You know that among the pagans their so-called rulers lord it over them and their great men make their authority felt. This is not to happen among you. No; anyone who wants to become great among you must be your servant and anyone who wants to be first among you must be slave to all. For the Son of Man himself did not come to be served but to serve, and to give his life as a ransom for many.' (Mk10:35-45)

For many in the group, the story of sin in this text is very true for our society in that so often we are like 'pagans'. Our 'so called rulers lord it over' us and our 'great men make their authority felt'. They shared their experience of individuals who used their positions as leaders of government, civil servants, police officers, professionals, 'to lord it over them' and 'make their authority felt'. In fact it is very common for young persons to deliberately choose professional careers in medicine and law, not because they wish to contribute to our society and country but because these are very highly paid professions with a high social profile. So, a career is assessed in terms of how much they can get from it, how much money, how much power.

The group asked the question: Who was Jesus for us? – who showed them by their words and actions that true leadership is not about lording over others and making their authority felt but it is really about service? Who spoke to them saying 'this situation is not to happen among you'?

Most of the group saw their parents and teachers as Jesus. They told of instances when they themselves lived this and having lived it, realized that it was true. They also remembered the times when they acted contrary to the values of this Gospel. Their reading and reflection of this text coincided with the national celebration of the Muslim festival of Eid-ul-Fitr and the Hindu festival of Divali. These celebrations also formed part of the sharing and reflection of the Gospel text. Many members of the group shared that this insight is fundamental to all these religions as evidenced by the lives of ordinary Hindus and Muslims in our country. They also celebrated great people of these religious traditions – the deceased ex-President of Trinidad, Noor Hassanali, a devout Muslim and a very humble man who lived this understanding of leadership as service throughout an illustrious career as lawyer, judge, Chief Justice and President. In the wider world they celebrated the great Hindu leader, Mahatma Gandhi, as well as the Muslim, Mohammed Yunus, who was awarded that year's Nobel Peace Prize for the work that he has done among the poor and vulnerable. His Grameen Movement is well known in Trinidad – introduced by Sister Rosario Hackshaw, a Catholic nun, and herself a longtime *lectio* practitioner, who is heavily involved in development work with the rural poor. She went to Bangladesh to study with Yunis. It has had a wide positive impact on our people in Trinidad through the development of similar micro-credit and micro-funding programmes.

This wider awareness helps the members of the group to understand at a very deep level, that the Gospel is not only for the local Catholic community, but for our entire society, regardless of race or religion. It applies to everyone, of any religion and at any moment in history. And what wisdom did they discover through their reflection? That we are at our best when we give of ourselves and it is only then that we become who God has called us to be.

These reflections led the group into prayer:

Lord, we thank you for your Word today. We thank you for all the people in our lives: our parents, teachers, NGO leaders, who, like Jesus, call us to them and say to us that we must not be like the pagans whose so-called rulers lord it over them and whose great men make their authority felt.

We thank you that instead, they taught us by word and example, that anyone who wants to become great amongst us must be our servant and anyone who wants to be first amongst us must be slave to all.

We thank you for all the people who have lived this – our parents, our ex-President Noor Hassanali, great leaders like Mahatma Gandhi and others of all races and religions who have lived this understanding of leadership as service.

Forgive us when we are carried away by our own ambition and sense of personal power, when we deliberately seek to gain from our advancement by using our positions as civil servants, doctors and lawyers, to make life difficult for others, when as leaders of government we make agreements and enact laws that disempower the poor and powerless and destroy our environment. At these times we are like the pagans.

Instead, Lord, help us to know that anyone who wants to be great among us must be our servant and anyone who wants to be first among us, must be slave to all. For the Son of Man himself did not come to be served, but to serve and to give his life as a ransom for many. Amen.

This is *lectio divina* in practice – the dynamic of Reading, Reflection and Prayer.

This group is very mature in their practice of *lectio divina*. Over the years it has given them a new vision of life that is broad and magnanimous. It has helped them to grow in confidence, to see their lives as valuable, to develop a generosity of spirit – the spirit of Jesus, to be more compassionate and not condemning both of themselves and of others. It has helped them to be patient with themselves and with life. They have come to love the text, to stay with and savor words and phrases. To them the text is always Good News, it always raises the lowly, it is never moralizing, it is not a big stick to beat others with, it is not a source of a message or a teaching.

The Gospel text has given them hope, they have learnt that good will always have the final say, that the story of grace in our lives is always the deeper, truer story and that God is alive in the world. It has also helped them to recognize and relate to the historical Jesus as someone who lived in a particular place and time in history, who was fully immersed and involved in his own time as a maker of history, who was open to learning from his experiences so that he grew in wisdom and grace as he made his own journey through life.

Such recognition continues to challenge them to be as fully immersed in our own time. It also helps them to recognize that he continues to engage them in dialogue through the events of their lives.

THE METHOD

This group, as well as many other parish groups throughout Trinidad and Tobago, was introduced to the method of *lectio divina* by Fr Michel de Verteuil, C.S.Sp. Fr. Michel's long engagement with *lectio divina* began more than 25 years ago when after twelve years of teaching theology in the Regional Seminary, he was given the responsibility for lay theological formation in the Archdiocese. Initially he thought that it was just a matter of changing students (members of a parish community rather than seminarians) and the setting (the parish rather than the classroom). However, he soon realized that teaching lay persons was a far cry from teaching seminarians. Many of them did not have a secondary, far less tertiary, education and found it difficult to grasp abstract concepts. They wanted to know how to be good parents, teachers, friends, leaders in their communities – how to live Gospel values in the world. A lot of what he was teaching them was not making any difference to their lives and they had very little to hold on to after his sessions with them were finished. After much searching he found the method he was looking for – *lectio divina* – the dominant theological method practised in the early centuries of the Church.

The Bible Story and Our Story

Lectio divina is based on the specific understanding of the Scriptures as story. This goes against what has prevailed in our Church for many centuries. The text has been seen as containing a message or a teaching and once we get this, the text has achieved its purpose. However, in *lectio divina* we read the text, the Bible story, in dialogue with our story, our personal experience. We love the text, we linger over it, we read it aloud over and over, we hear the words of the text, we let it remain with us.

Gradually we recognize the text. We find that we have lived these events ourselves or have seen them lived by others who have touched our lives for good or for ill. Reading the text becomes an experience of homecoming and a lifting up. We find ourselves caught up in the story of God's people, 'fellow citizens with the saints'. It also allows the text to become a place of personal encounter with God. In this respect, *lectio divina* is truly radical as it allows God to engage anyone in dialogue, even the lowliest in the eyes of the world.

Lectio divina, like story telling, is a form of imaginative communication. It teaches not directly, but by changing the consciousness of those who practise it so that we see people and life differently. By identifying ourselves with God's people – Jesus, the Good Samaritan, the prophets and the great men and women of the Bible, we find ourselves adopting their attitudes. We also recognize ourselves in the bad characters of the text, *e.g.*, the Pharisees, the unjust judge, the pagans whose leaders lord it over them, and find that we want to give up those attitudes and values.

In the text, therefore, we discover the double reality of every human person – a story of sin and a story of grace, which is the deeper truth of the person. Reflecting on the text leads spontaneously into prayer: thanksgiving when we have lived our story of grace, humility that the story of sin is alive and petition that the story of grace will prevail. Finally, through reading and reflecting on the text, we allow God, God alive in the text, to lead us into wisdom, a wisdom that gives us his perspective on all aspects of life, not only our personal relationships but our work, our society, the world.

Staying with the Sunday Lectionary

Lectio Divina is best practised with the Church's Sunday lectionary. This is how it is done in Trinidad. By being faithful to the lectionary, parish and community groups experience themselves in communion with the Church and through the Church, with all humanity, sharing the grace and sin of their contemporaries.

In the method of *lectio divina* as developed by Fr Michel, once the introductory sessions are completed, those who had attended the training sessions are left to continue on their own. Individuals are encouraged to form groups for their weekly meeting and to trust themselves, the text and the method. Every group will be a microcosm of the parish with members who are fundamentalist or self-righteous. However, it is our experience that the group usually corrects itself. While the focus is generally on the Gospel texts of Ordinary Time, most parishes and institutions, *e.g.*, the Bible School, offer additional courses or retreats that focus specifically on the seasons of the Church Year – Advent, Lent, Easter.

The fact that the Sunday Lectionary is used means that everyone has a common theological text at hand at very little cost. In addition, there is a certain amount of support for this as the weekly Catholic newspaper, the *Catholic News*, carries both the Sunday text and a reflection on it that may help readers to enter and engage with the text. It also gives introductions to the seasons as well as commentaries on the Gospel and background on the writer. In addition, the philosophy of the *Catholic News* draws upon *lectio divina* as evidenced, for example, by the editorial.

PRACTICE AND FRUITS OF *LECTIO DIVINA*

Over time, by following the Sunday Lectionary, practitioners of *lectio divina* gain a greater sense of ownership of the Church as they no longer perceive it as belonging only to the priests or to the Bible experts. As a result, many people have become encouraged to involve themselves in the life of the Church community as catechists, lectors, RCIA sponsors, and lay ministers.

Our experience of *lectio divina* according to the method of Fr Michel has taught us that theological education is about walking with each other and discovering and telling our stories, being healed and coming to wholeness, discovering our greatness, knowing for ourselves that our stories are true and worthwhile and sacred because they are part of the sacred history that is the Scripture.

This is very important because many in our society are trained to forget – to put the past, both good and bad, but especially bad, behind us and move on. One of the first fruits of *lectio* is that we remember and reclaim our stories. This helps us to heal, to bring resolution to our lives, and sometimes, for the first time, to start taking responsibility for our lives. We also come to recognize not only the God who has always been with us but also who we truly are. We begin to see that where we live is a holy place. It may be a depressed area, looked down on by the rest of society, but the people who live there are able to recognize Jesus living among them. Because of this, many ordinary people have come to see life through the perspective of the wisdom of God and have been empowered to live creatively in their communities, their parishes and in the wider society. This is tremendously important for our Caribbean people because our culture gives us, especially the poor, a very negative image of themselves.

Also *lectio divina*, has helped many to discover the stories of grace lived by their ancestors, which in the Caribbean means mainly African and Asian ancestors who came to these islands as slaves or indentured labourers. This is tremendously important as our history teaches us to look down on our ancestors. Now through *lectio divina*, we can all celebrate our ancestors.

Over the years, *lectio divina* has spread through the life of the local Church. Ordinary people are introduced to it though courses at Bible School as well as the annual Archdiocesan Summer Liturgy School. It forms the basis of the catechumen's journey through the RCIA, it is a method often used for retreats, It is practised by priests and religious in preparation for their homilies, as well as lay persons.

Priests and their Sunday Sermons

The practice of *lectio divina* develops and matures most effectively when introductory engagements are followed through by regular weekly practice within the support structure of a group. Every week, for the last 25 years, a group of priests have been meeting with Fr Michel to prepare their Sunday homily. They start by looking back at their homilies of the previous Sunday. What did it do for them personally? Did it move them? Did they enjoy it? What kind of feedback, if any, did they get from their congregation? They then move on to prepare the following Sunday's homily together. It is their experience that *lectio divina* has helped them. Over the years, the group has widened to include a religious sister who has pastoral care of a parish and three women who are involved in parish *lectio* groups. These weekly meetings are occasions for doing theology, preparing homilies, growing spiritually and becoming friends. This is *lectio divina* at its best.

For Everyone

It is our experience that everyone, no matter his or her situation, standard of education, or social status, can do *lectio divina*. There will be those who are very good at it and those who will find it difficult. Sometimes, this is because the person has only ever been exposed to a fundamentalist approach to the Bible. Sometimes, people may have hidden or deeply buried memories they do not want to access. We need to be patient and honest with ourselves and to bear in mind that *lectio divina* is an exercise of the heart and spirit, not the head.

Lectio divina can occur in surprising contexts. A member of a parish *lectio* group who facilitates a monthly NGO forum, has used the method of *lectio divina* to inspire the members of this forum and to generate the values that create the development agenda within which they operate. Trinidad has a multi-ethnic and multi-religious population and, as a result, there is great respect and tolerance for all religious traditions. It is the norm for any meeting to start with a religious activity – a prayer, a reflection, a ritual. The members of this NGO forum reflect the full religious spectrum of Trinidad – Catholic, Christian, Hindu, Muslim, Spiritual Baptist – yet they have got into the habit of starting off their monthly meeting with *lectio divina* under the direction of their facilitator. They read and reflect on the text from the perspective of their work in the NGO sector. Most, including the non-Christian groups see Jesus as a wise person, a teacher of wisdom and a role model for the NGO sector.

A memorable example of the group's reflections was on the Gospel text in which the Pharisees challenge the disciples of Jesus because 'a number of tax collectors and sinners came to sit at the table with Jesus and his disciples'. This Gospel triggered a vigorous discussion among members about the experiences of exclusion and marginalisation in their focus areas. At the end, one of the participants, a woman of the Spiritual Baptist faith whose members have had a long history of dis-empowerment and isolation in our country, summed it up by saying that she now had a much clearer perspective on the role of the NGO sector – to work toward the day when all people in our country can sit and eat at the same table. Isn't that marvellous?

Another time, a meeting of this group coincided with the worldwide commemoration of two events – the 250th anniversary of Mozart and the liberation of Auschwitz. The text of the following Sunday told the story of Jesus, seen as a very good man, confronting a man in the syna-gogue of Capernaum who is possessed by an unclean spirit. Reflecting on the text with the background of these two world events reminded the group that good and evil are not abstract concepts. They are real, they operate at both individual and institutional level, and have real effects on people. Humanity has the capacity for both great good and great evil. Members reflected that Mozart and the beautiful music he composed, exemplified humanity at its best – the heights of creativity and beauty that an individual can achieve if given the opportunity, the joy that one person can bring into the world, the positive difference that one person can make. On the other hand, they saw Auschwitz as an extreme example of institutionalized evil and individual depravity.

Members of the NGO forum reflected that the Gospel text told the story of a confrontation between Good and Evil. They realized that a lot of the development work they did, was, at some level, promoting and facilitating the emergence of good and confronting and destroying evil: both the evil that emerges from individual abuse and disinterest as well as institutionalized evil in the systems, rules and laws that conspire to impoverish, dis-empower and marginalize many individuals and communities in our society They shared many concrete ways in which they acted like Jesus in the synagogue in Capernaum, by 'teaching with authority' by speaking out on social and environmental issues and identifying priorities for the sector, and 'calling forth unclean spirits' through interventions that built capacity, reduced illiteracy, addressed various forms of abuse, neglect and exploitation and challenged the forces that help evil in the world. This meeting was in preparation for the group's annual strategic planning. They felt that their reflection on this text gave them a clear context within which to set their priorities for the year.

A FINAL WORD FROM THE *LECTIO DIVINA* GROUP IN ARIMA

The Arima group likened their experience of the method of Fr Michel to the sower going out to sow. It is a method that is implicitly generous and trusting. Just as the sower does not sow only on rich soil, similarly the method of *lectio divina* does not require someone to be highly educated, to be widely read, even to be Catholic, as shown by the experience of the NGO worker. Anyone and everyone can access the text through *lectio divina*. In fact, like Arima, many of the people in *lectio divina* groups in parishes or in RCIA programmes in Trinidad and Tobago are very ordinary individuals with very basic education. The sower – what a wonderful symbol of generosity. He does not calculate the results, the problems or the failure rate. He just sows. When the seed germinates, it germinates.

Lectio divina is like this: it is generous, it is not result-oriented. It waits on people. When insight or understanding comes, it comes. But because of this it is not an easy way. The easy way is to give the message, information, a teaching. It is much harder and more challenging to wait on people, even to wait on yourself – everyone coming to insight and understanding in their own way and time. This is not man's way but it is certainly God's way. It mirrors the spirit of Jesus. Do you think that Jesus would have sown any seed if he had sat down to calculate his results?

The Liberating Reading of the Bible in the Base Ecclesial Communities in Brazil

CARLOS MESTERS, O.CARM.

THIS ARTICLE reflects on our practice in the Centre for Biblical Studies (CEBI)[1] and in the Base Ecclesial Communities in Brazil, where reading the Bible has a liberating effect. Although they are only a minority, their influence in the life of the wider Church is very significant.

I want to start with ten statements that list the characteristics of a liberating reading of the Bible:

1. The Bible is the Word of God.
2. Bible and life are closely connected.
3. God is with us is the central truth that people discover.
4. What was distant is now close to us
5. The Bible is 'our book,' source of critical awareness
6. The people find the meaning of life with the help of the Bible
7. The way of reading the Bible is Good News for the poor
8. There are certain conditions for seeing the connections between Bible and life.
9. The method is an activity that involves people.
10. There has to be an atmosphere of faith and mutual love.

---

1. The Centre for Biblical Studies (CEBI) is an ecumenical entity, set up in 1977, to articulate, spread and legitimise the reading of the Bible that the people do in their communities. Its objective is to promote a liberating reading of the Bible at the service of a pastoral engagement among the people in the Christian communities.

Carlos Mesters OCARM has spent much of his life in Brazil, teaching Scripture in a seminary and working with basic Christian communities. He is the author of several books, especially on the application of Scripture to life.

This article was translated from the Portuguese by Sister Colm McCool OP and Sister Elizabeth Delaney OP, Bom Sucesso, Lisbon.

BACKGROUND

Many factors contributed to the discovery of this type of Bible reading. We will consider how the upheavals of the twentieth century and renewal in the Churches led to a renewed interest in the Bible. In Brazil, these factors combined with the oppression of the people to create a thirst for biblical spirituality. These factors were not present in isolation, but were shaped by the Holy Spirit.

A New Way of Looking at God's Revelation and the Bible

The great changes in the history of the human race in the nineteenth and twentieth centuries led Christians from the different Churches to see reality and the Bible in a different light. For example, the experience of Rudolf Bultmann as a chaplain in the trenches in the First World War, 1914-1918 led him to approach the Bible in a new way that influenced twentieth century biblical exegesis in practically all the Churches.

In Belgium, the critical situation between the two world wars and the experience of living with manual labourers led Father Joseph Cardijn to devise the See, Judge, Act method. Before seeking to know what God said in the past, we have to see the situation of people to-day and become aware of their problems. Next, with the help of texts from the Bible and the tradition of the Churches, we try to judge the situation. This means that, soon, the Word of God is seen to come, not just from the Bible, but also, and especially from the actual facts illuminated by the Bible and by tradition. And it is these facts which thus become vehicles for the transmission of the Word and of the call of God and which lead us to ACT in a different way. This method, see / judge /act, had a very great influence on the renewal movements in the Catholic Church in Brazil in the 1950s and 1960s, especially in the various sectors of Catholic Action – Young Catholic Youth, Young Catholic Students, Young Catholic University Students, Young Catholic Farm Workers. It gave rise to a change in the way people sought to know God's will and made possible a more ecumenical and less confessional attitude among people.

In the United States, the political involvement of N.K. Gottwald in the struggle against the war in Vietnam had a profound influence on the way he re-read and interpreted the origin and formation of the People of God. His writings, especially the book, *The Tribes of Yahweh*, had a great influence on those who studied the Bible in Brazil, particularly with respect to the method of approaching and interpreting Exodus.

In Latin America, in the 1960s and 1970s, the political commitment of many Christians had, and continues to have, deep repercussions on their way of reading and interpreting the Bible. The cruelty of the military dictatorships, in some cases carried out with the veiled support of the ecclesiastical authorities or in the name of Christian tradition, led the more aware to a new reading of the Bible in defence of life – a more liberating and more ecumenical reading, preventing the Word of God from being manipulated so as to legitimise the oppression and exploitation of the people.

Renewal in the Churches Leads to a Renewed Interest in the Bible.

After the upheaval of the wars of 1914-18 and 1939-45 most Churches entered on a process of conversion and change. The new circumstances in which the human race found itself made it clear that a re-reading of matters of faith was necessary, in view of the different experiences of God and of life that had arisen. This change or conversion took place in different ways in different Churches and different countries.

In the Catholic Church in Brazil, for example, the document, *Dei Verbum* of the Second Vatican Council and its application to Latin America by the Bishops' Conferences at Medellín and Puebla confirmed that God continues to speak today, speaking to us through events and people, and that we can discover this divine message with the help of the written Word of God in the Bible.

After the Second Vatican Council, Catholics became more interested in the Bible, and through various channels it came more and more into the hands of the people. The renewal of the liturgy, in which the Bible would be read in the vernacular, brought the word of God much closer to the people. Further, in the 1950s Scripture scholar João José Pedreira de Castro, O.F.M., read the signs of the times and realized the need to bring the Bible closer to the people. With this in view he translated the Maredsous Bible into Portuguese, now in more than 150 successive editions and known as the Ave Maria Bible. Thirdly, the members of the League of Biblical Studies (LEB) succeeded in making a translation of the Bible directly from the original sources, now published by Editora Loyola. They also organized biblical weeks in every district. Finally, the arrival of evangelical missionary Churches in Brazil in the first half of the twentieth century, coming mostly from the United States, awakened many Catholics the importance of the Word of God. Initially there was a defensive reaction against what some called 'the Protestant threat'. Bit by bit however it was seen as one of God's greatest graces.

The Situation of the People, the Military Coup and the Rise of Bible Circles

The situation of the people was (and continues to be) one of abandonment, oppression and exploitation. Hence, there was a whole political effort to raise awareness in order to make change possible. Members of various sectors of Catholic Action took an active part in this work. They managed to form a group, *Ação Popular* (Popular Action), which had a very important political approach. However, the military coup of 1964 showed, indirectly, that political awareness among the people had not been what the leaders of the political opposition imagined. The reaction against the military that they hoped for, did not happen. It became clear that more intense and more patient work needed to be done with the people, with greater respect for their religion, their culture and their way of life.

Thus from about the middle of the 1960s, a more basic kind of work began among the poor, and the Base Ecclesial Communities were the result. At a time of persecution and ideological control the Churches opened a space where opposition could be articulated, with a certain freedom. For that very reason, they suffered political repression. It is enough to recall the names of Dom Helder Câmara, Dom Pedro Casaldáliga, Father Henrique, Santo Dias, Margarida Alves and many other leaders, religious and lay – persecuted, imprisoned, tortured and assassinated.

From the need for pastoral activity that would be more intense and more respectful, Bible Circles started up everywhere. The method used in the Bible Circles took into account, on the one hand, the experience gained in the groups of Catholic Action with their see/ judge/act methodology along with the teaching of Paulo Freire on the pedagogy of the oppressed, and, on the other, the tradition of the Gospels themselves. The way of reading the Bible in the Base Ecclesial

Communities closely resembled the method suggested by the Gospel of St Luke in the Emmaus story. The process of interpretation followed by Jesus has the same three steps that also make up the method adopted by the poor people in the Bible Circles of the Base Ecclesial Communities: (1) begin with the reality of life (Lk 24:13-24); (2) use a text from the Bible (Lk 24:25-27); (3) celebrate and share in the community (Lk 24:28-32).

Jesus met the two friends in a situation of fear and flight, of unbelief and despair. They were running away. The forces of death, the cross, had put an end to all hope for them. Jesus came and walked with them, listened to their conversation and asked: 'What are you talking about?' The dominant ideology kept them from really understanding and exercising their critical faculty. 'We had hoped that he was the one to redeem Israel, but ....' (Lk 24:21)

This is the first step: approach people, listen to their real situation, their problems; know how to ask questions that will help them to look at their actual situation in a more critical way.

Jesus used the Bible, not to give a Bible class, but to throw light on a problem that was making his two friends suffer and, in this way, to interpret the situation in which they were living. With the help of the Bible, he positioned them within God's plan and showed them that their story had not escaped from God's hand.

The second step is this: with the help of the Bible, to throw light on the situations and transform the cross, sign of death, into a sign of life and hope. Thus what was preventing them from understanding now became light and strength on their journey.

The Bible, of itself, may not open our eyes, but it makes our hearts burn within us. (Lk 24:32). What opened the eyes of the two friends and made them aware of the presence of Jesus was the breaking of the bread, the act of sharing together, the celebration. The moment they recognised him, Jesus disappeared. Then they themselves experienced the resurrection: They were born again and began walking on their own.

The third step is this: to know how to create a prayerful atmosphere of faith and mutual love where the Spirit can act and lead us to grasp the meaning of what Jesus is saying. It is above all at this point in the celebration that the practice of the communities helped all concerned to find again the ancient well of Tradition and to drink from it.

The result was that they were able to rise again and return to Jerusalem (Lk. 24:33-35) where the forces of death, which killed Jesus, were still active, but where now the forces of life were manifest in the sharing of Resurrection. Courage, instead of fear. Return, instead of flight. Faith, instead of disbelief. Hope, instead of despair. A critical conscience instead of fatalism when confronted by power. Freedom, instead of oppression. In a word, life instead of death! Instead of the bad news of Jesus' death, the Good News of his Resurrection. This should be the result of reading the Bible: to experience the living presence of Jesus and his Spirit in our midst. It is he who will open our eyes to the Bible and to reality and lead us to share the experience of Resurrection, which is what happens to this day in our community meetings.

The Action of the Holy Spirit

We have seen the three elements that help us to understand the reality of what is going on in our midst; there is a fourth element, the most important of all, which can be neither measured nor defined, but which acts through all the other elements. It is the action of the Holy Spirit who can never be caught in the act but who, invisibly, is acting in this journey and is directing it. 'If anyone has ears to hear, let him listen to what the Spirit is saying to the churches' (Rev 2,:7,11, 17, 29; 3:6, 13, 22)

In this way from the '60s and '70s onward, the people began to read the Bible. In just a few years the Bible Circles spread throughout Brazil, a sign that they were answering a real need. Only the Holy Spirit knows how many Bible Circles there are at present. They were, and continue to be, the beginning of a new way of being Church.

THREE STAGES OF DEVELOPMENT

During these years three aspects of popular interpretation appeared, simultaneous and intermingled. These aspects are: knowing the Bible; creating community; serving the people.

Knowing the Bible – Teaching

The process of knowing the Bible better began in the nineteenth century, with the renewal work of European exegetes, both Protestant and Catholic. The new discoveries brought new knowledge, opening a new window on the biblical texts and the context of their origin.

The desire to know the Bible better stimulated many people to read it more frequently. In the Catholic Church, the renewal in exegesis, the encyclicals of Leo XII, Benedict XV and Pius XII, the new translation of the Bible and the work of exegetes all brought the Bible closer to the people. As well as that, in Brazil, as we have already mentioned, what helped to arouse in Catholics a greater interest in the Bible was the missionary zeal of the Evangelical Churches.

On every side there were Bible weeks, Bible courses, Bible schools, big and small, Bible gymkhanas and marathons, and many other movements and initiatives aimed at spreading knowledge of the Bible and encouraging people to read it. The Bible Month was celebrated for more than 25 years and is continued to the present day in many places. The Good News Movement (MOBON) was initially concerned with the apologetics needed to defend Catholicism against the growing influence of the Evangelical Churches. Now, it is one of the most widely spread movements of liberating evangelization and is responsible for more than 15,000 groups in various States of Brazil. It is difficult to remember and list all the initiatives that the creativity of the people invented in order to spread the reading and the knowledge of the Bible.

Creating Community – Celebrating

As the Word of God became known, it produced its fruits. The first fruit was to draw people together and create community. Popular biblical weeks, the circulation of the Bible in the vernacular, courses, meetings, training sessions, innumerable groups and Bible Circles, Bible months, the Good News movement: all produced a very great enthusiasm in the community, centred on the Word of God. The renewal of the liturgy meant that celebrations of the Word became more frequent and more fervent.

The Base Ecclesial Communities were established and grew in number, and this in turn gave rise everywhere to Bible Circles, reflection groups, Gospel groups, prayer groups. In the beginning of the 1970s we had the initiative of Inter-Church Base Communities which took place periodically and which in the year 2000 celebrated the tenth

Interchurch assembly in Porto Seguro, Bahia. The communitarian dimension brought about a renewal in various parishes that later came to organize themselves into a community of communities.

Here we should mention the fact that large numbers left the traditional Churches for the Pentecostal groups, due to socio–economic changes over the last 50s years. For the first half of the twentieth century, about 75% of the population of Brazil lived in rural areas. Industrialization and the rural exodus produced a radical change: by 2001, 82% of the population lived in the cities, only 18% in the country. What before seemed impossible, now became normal: the most important moral authority that, in Brazil, guided peoples' consciences, was the Catholic Church. In the little towns of the interior of Brazil, the parish priest exercised considerable spiritual power. It was only with great difficulty that people could challenge or break away from this traditional system. Today, in the name of a communitarian experience in the Pentecostal groups on the outskirts of the big cities, millions of Brazilians have broken away from what was once the greatest moral authority. However contradictory and ambivalent this fact may appear, it has, nevertheless, a positive dimension: in the name of the word of God and of an encounter with Jesus, the people have the courage to break away and embark on new ways which, perhaps, are not really new, but which are different and have a profound communitarian dimension.

Serving the People – Transformation

From 1968 on, another step was taken. Knowledge of the Bible and concern for establishing community met their objective which is service of the people. Without either the money or the time to read books about the Bible, the poor in their communities and in the Bible Circles began to read the Bible itself, using the only criterion they knew – their life of faith lived in community and their life of suffering as an oppressed people. Reading the Bible from this point of view, they discovered in it what they had not seen before: a story of oppression similar to what they themselves suffered, a story of struggle for the same values that they are still seeking today: land, justice, sharing, brotherhood, a truly human life. The result of this liberating practice was given expression in Liberation Theology which endeavoured to systematize the new experience of life in the communities.

This was a period in which the political dimension of faith began to be emphasized. In the Catholic Church after the Second Vatican Council and, especially after the episcopal conference of Medellín (1968) there was an important evolution. Faced with the dramatic situation of the Indians (indigenous Americans) the Missionary Council for Indians (CIMI) was set up. In relation to the worsening situation of the farm workers, the Pastoral Commission for the Land (CPT) was formed. To remedy the situation of the factory workers, the Pastoral Commission for Factory Workers (CPO) was initiated. For the fishermen, there was the Pastoral Commission for Fishermen (CPP). These new pastoral initiatives have one thing in common: they arose because of a renewed faith in Jesus, and, like Jesus, they defend life, they are ecumenical, they upset the established order, they provoke controversy. All this reveals the evolution taking place in the consciousness the Churches have of themselves and their mission: to struggle in defence of the threatened life of their people. It was in the same period (the 1970s), that the Ecumenical Centre for Bible Studies (CEBI) emerged, to provide a pastoral approach from among the people (*Pastoral Popular*) to put shape upon, express, deepen, spread and legitimise the reading of the Bible which the people were carrying out in their communities.

Here we must remember the martyrs who gave their lives for the cause of justice and brotherhood. Thus, just as the author of the Letter to the Hebrews recalls the heroes of faith (Heb 11:1-40), the *Latin American Calendar*, every year, recalls the memory of thousands and thousands of Latin American martyrs, men, women and children, lay people and religious, known and unknown, who imitated Jesus as he said, 'I have come so that they may have life and have it to the full'. (Jn 10:10)

THE INTERNAL DYNAMICS
OF THE PROCESS OF INTERPRETATION

In the manner in which the communities read the Bible, in spite of the differences in each country or each region, there is a method whose basic characteristics are common to all. A method is much more than a set of techniques and dynamics. It is an attitude towards the

Bible and towards life. The method of the poor has three dimensions:

1. The present situation: The poor bring to the Bible the problems of their own lives. They read the Bible in the context of their own struggle and the reality of their present situation.

2. The community: Their reading is done in community. It is, above all, a reading in common, a practice of prayer, an act of faith.

3. The text: Their reading is done in obedience: they respect the text and set themselves to listen to what God has to say, ready to change if he asks them.

These three dimensions (Text, Community, Reality) relate to one another towards the same objective: to listen to God today. They bring up to date in their own way the same method that may be detected in the story of the disciples on the road to Emmaus (Lk. 24:13-35). They are like three aspects or stages of one and the same interpretive attitude towards the Bible. There is an interior dynamic that marks the popular interpretation: Knowing the Bible leads to people living together in community; living together in community leads to serving the people; serving the people, in turn, leads to desiring a deeper understanding of the context in which the Bible originated, and so on. It is a never-ending dynamic. With these three aspects, one is born from the other and leads to the other.

The diagram makes clear what we are trying to say.

It does not matter from which of these three aspects the process of interpretation begins. That depends on the situation, the history, the culture and the particular interest of the community or the group. What is important is to understand that one aspect is incomplete without the other two.

Generally, in all communities, there are people who identify with one or the other of these three aspects: people who want to get to know the Bible and are now more interested in study; those who are more insistent on the importance of community and its internal workings; people who are more concerned about transforming the reality, the actual situation serving the people in politics and in the popular movements.

All this produces tensions in the various groups and in their particular interests. These tensions are healthy and fruitful. For example, in some places the more intense political action of the last few years demands, now, a deeper knowledge of the biblical text and the social context, out of which this text arose, and a more intense effort to live out in community the spirituality of liberation. In other places the communitarian living went as far as it could go and now demands a more committed activity in the popular movements.

The tensions can help to create a balance that enhances the interpretation of the Bible and prevents it from becoming one-sided. Sometimes, however, these tensions are negative and can lead one of these three aspects closing in on itself and excluding the other two. The process of popular interpretation is often tense and full of conflict, running the risk of moving back instead of forward.

When the community reaches the objective of one of these aspects (knowing, living or transforming) some members of it, out of fidelity to the Word, want to advance and take another step forward, while others in the name of the same fidelity, refuse to open up further. These are moments of crisis and also of grace. The group that wants to advance is not always the winner.

All the pastoral movements use the Bible and learn. Fundamentalists, on the other hand, in the name of the same Bible, refuse to accept the interpretation and the opening towards reality. In some places, Bible groups became closed in on themselves and on the letter (the literal sense) of the Bible. These became the most conservative groups in the parish. Even the exegete can run the risk of being locked into the liberal and even progressive study of the biblical text, while at the same time, finding himself at the service of the conservative forces of oppression.

Some movements close themselves into the community aspect. Whether mystic or charismatic, they refuse to be open to the social and political aspects. They are open to the service of the poor (and that's not little) but not to the aspect of transformation and liberation. They do not trouble the conscience of the oppressors and do not upset the system in which we live.

There can also a closing-in on the opposite side, though this is less frequent. It can happen that a community which has arrived at a high degree of awareness and of political commitment begins to attach less importance to community living, to personal devotions, to pilgrimages and processions. All this, in their view, can be relatively easily manipulated by the dominant ideology. And so they conclude, all too hastily, that such practices do not make for transformation. Hence, they run the risk of locking themselves into the social aspect, into politics, into the service of the people, forgetting the spiritual dimension and the mystical aspect of community living.

Although understandable, such tendencies to become locked-in to one or other aspect are unfortunate, because no one of the three has real meaning on it own. To overcome this danger, it is important to maintain dialogue. Where the human word flows freely and uncensored, the word of God generates freedom.

ORIGINALITY AND CHANGE

Within the way in which the poor interpret the Bible there is something original that may be very far-reaching for the life of the Churches. Something new which is also old and which takes up again some basic values of the common Tradition. Here are seven points, which in one way or another, mark the journey.

1. The aim of interpretation is not to collect information about the past, but rather to clarify the present with the help of the light of the presence of God-with-us, the liberating God: it is to interpret life with the help of the Bible. People re-discover themselves in acquiring a new vision of Revelation.

2. The subject of interpretation is not now the Bible scholar, the exegete. Interpreting is an activity that belongs to the community in which everyone has a role, each in accordance with his or her own ability, including the Bible scholar who has a very special role. Therefore, it is important not only to keep in mind the faith of the community, but also to be an effective part of a living community and to seek the meaning that will be relevant to that community. This kind of active belonging will exercise a critical influence on the contribution of the

Bible scholar who will then be found to be increasingly at the service of the community. The same might be said about theology. As a result of changes taking place in the world, the theology of liberation entered a period of questioning and is now in a period of revision. On the other hand, it could be said that the way the people read the Bible is not in crisis, but is growing on all sides: the subject of this way of reading is not the Bible scholar, but more the people in the base ecclesial communities.

3. The social condition where the interpretation takes place is among the poor, the excluded and the marginalized. This changes the viewpoint. Very often, for want of a more critical social conscience, the interpreter is the victim of ideological prejudices, and without realizing it, uses the Bible to legitimise a a dehumanising system of oppression.

4. The way of reading that relates the Bible to life is ecumenical and liberating. An ecumenical reading does not mean that Catholics and Protestants discuss their differences in order to arrive at a common conclusion. That could be a consequence. The most ecumenical thing we have is the life that God gave us. Here in Latin America the life of a great part of the population is in danger – it is not really life. Ecumenical reading means interpreting the Bible in defence of life and not in defence of our distinct institutions and different confessions. In the actual situation in which the peoples of Latin America live, a reading in defence of life must necessarily be liberating. By that very fact, it leads to conflict. It becomes a sign of contradiction. In order to be ecumenical and liberating, it goes beyond the frontiers of our institutions and it is now read from the point of view of different marginalized groups – Negroes, Indians, women, homosexuals. The basic criterion is no longer a particular Church, but life itself, as seen through the eyes of race, type, culture, class. Or, perhaps, the criterion is to explain the mystery of the Church as defined by Paul. 'For all of you who were baptized into Christ have clothed yourselves with Christ. There is neither Jew nor Greek, there is neither male nor female, for you are all one in Christ Jesus.' (Gal 3:27-28).

5. The major problem with us is not, as in Europe, that the faith is in danger because of secularisation. It is rather that life is in serious danger of being eliminated and dehumanised because of an economic

system that is unjust and exclusive. And, worse still, the Bible itself runs the risk of being used to legitimise idols. The Bible was used to legitimise the Conquest of the Americas, the politics of apartheid, of military dictatorships and of repression. One of the greatest repressors and torturers used to say: 'My bedside reading is the Gospel of St Matthew'. And General Pinochet always compared himself to Moses, liberator of his people. Popular interpretation reveals and denounces this kind of manipulation.

6. The method and the dynamics used by the poor in their meetings, are simple. They do not use intellectual discursive language; they relate aspects of life as it is and use comparisons. Popular language functions by means of the association of ideas. Its first concern is not to inform but to discover. In all this the pedagogical method of the oppressed, identified by Paulo Freire, has been a great help.

7. The function and the limits of the Bible appear more clearly. The limits are these: The Bible is not an end in itself, but it is at the service of the interpretation of life. By itself it does not work and does not succeed in opening our eyes. What does open our eyes is the breaking of bread, the communitarian gesture. The Bible must be interpreted within a wider context, which takes into account the community and the reality of life. The Bible is like the heart: when it is taken out of the body of the community and the life of the people, it dies and causes death!

NEW WAYS APPEAR: NEW PROBLEMS ARISE

A Gender-based Reading

Gender-sensitive reading questions and relativises the age-old male-oriented way of reading practised by the Churches and maintaining their patriarchal system. It cannot be discounted as a passing phenomenon or as one of the many exegetical curiosities of no great consequence. It is one of the most important characteristics which have emerged from the peoples' reading of the Bible. Its importance is much greater than might appear at first sight. In Brazil it has an even greater importance because of the overwhelming majority of women who take an active part in the Bible groups and sustain the peoples' struggle in many places. In the CEBI there is a great number of assistants who have been trained in recent years and who are studying the gender–based reading not as a new sector, but as a characteristic which has to be part and parcel of all the reading which we do.

How Can We Face the Reality of Fundamentalism?

In the mass-meetings promoted by the television networks, singing priests appear. In the Bible meetings organized by the CEBI, open to people from different sectors of the life of the Churches, the following appears more and more frequently. The study and interpretation of the Bible are carried out clearly in a liberating direction. But in the celebrations, when the people converse, or when they ask questions, a different kind of interpretation appears, in which fundamentalism is mixed with liberation theology. This happens especially with young people. How can we explain this phenomenon? Where does it come from? From contact with the conservative position, the charismatic section, the Pentecostals? Could it arise, perhaps, from the deficiencies of the liberating attitude towards the Bible? Could it not arise also from something deeper which is changing in the sub-consciousness of the human race?

Fundamentalism does not exist only in the Christian Churches, but also in the other religions: Judaism, Islam, Buddhism. There are even forms of a secularised fundamentalism.

Fundamentalism is a danger. It separates the text from the rest of life and the history of the people and absolutizes it as the only manifestation of the Word of God. Life, the history of the people, of the community have nonothing to say about God and His will. Fundamentalism annuls the action of the Word of God in daily life. It is the total absence of a critical conscience. It distorts the meaning of the Bible and fosters moralism, individualism and spiritualism in interpreting it. It is an alienated vision which pleases the oppressors of the people, it also prevents the oppressed from becoming conscious of the iniquity of the system set up and maintained by the powerful.[2]

In the Catholic Church, for the first time, the document *The Use of*

2. Collection: *Tua Palavra é Vida, Vol I: A Leitura Orante da Bíblia*, Publicações CRB, 1990, p. 22.

the Bible in the Church, from the Pontifical Bible Commission, strongly criticizes fundamentalism as something prejudicial which does not sufficiently respect the meaning of the Bible.

In Search of Spirituality, and Our Method of Interpretation

At the moment one hears and feels everywhere a deepening desire for mysticism, or spirituality. The Bible can be the answer to this desire. Indeed, the Word of God has two fundamental dimensions: it brings light and strength. Its light can contribute towards clarifying ideas, unmasking false ideologies and forming a more critical conscience. A source of strength, it can stir people, give courage, bring joy, since it is the creative force that produces something new, helps people to grow, makes things happen, fosters love.

Unfortunately, too often in pastoral practice, these two aspects of the Word are separated. On the one hand, the charismatic movements; on the other, the liberation movements. The charismatics have a great deal of prayer, but they are very often wanting in critical vision and they tend towards a fundamentalist, moralising and individualist interpretation of the Bible. Hence, their prayer, often, has no real foundation in the text or in the reality of what is happening to people. The liberation movements, for their part, have a strong critical conscience but, at times, they lack perseverance and faith, when it is a question of dealing with human situations and relations between people which, looked at scientifically, do not contribute in any way towards the transformation of society. Sometimes, they have difficulty in recognising the usefulness of spending long hours in prayer without any immediate result.

There are already a number of important initiatives aimed at confronting and overcoming this problem. I mention the project *Your Word is Life* (the plan of biblical formation for religious organized the Conference of Religious of Brazil); the spirituality team of the Ecumenical Centre for Biblical Studies (CEBI); the initiative of the the National Conference of Bishops of Brazil (CNNB) to bring about a greater appreciation of the four Gospels and the Acts of the Apostles in preparation for the Jubilee of the New Millennium.

The Culture of Our People

In the Tucuman myth, which explains to the Indians of the Amazon regions the origin of evil in the world, the one who is guilty is not the woman but the man. During a Bible course in Bolivia in May 1991, the participants, almost all Aymaras, asked, 'Why use the Bible only? Our stories are nicer, less masochist and more familiar'.

The religions of Asia, older than ours, have been asking the same questions for years: What is the value of our history and of our culture? Could it be that they could not have value as our Old Testament, where we find the promises which God made to our ancestors and where our law exists as 'our disciplinarian before Christ came' (Gal 3:24)? The Gospel did not come to either eliminate or substitute for the Old Testament, but to complete it and explain its significance (Mt 5:17). The Old Testament of the people of Israel is the canon or the inspired norm that helps us to understand and reveal this deeper dimension of our culture and the history of our Old Testament. In this sense, the different approaches to indigenous, Negro and gender-sensitive reading are very important.

Need for a Greater Study of the Bible

The journey of the communities goes on and deepens. Gradually, from the heart of this practice of the people a new attitude towards interpretation arose, which is not new but indeed very old. It needs to be accepted as legitimate, both by the tradition of the Churches and by exegetical research. The reading which is done from the point of view of the poor and to promote the cause of the poor has its own demands. According as it advances, the desire for a more scientific investigation grows deeper. There are many assistants, both men and women, who would like to have some knowledge of the biblical languages: they would like to understand more fully the economic, social, political, social and ideological context out of which the Bible grew; they would like to raise within the Bible itself the questions which worry the people in the daily living out of their faith. There is a scarcity of academic assistants capable of responding to this need for the biblical formation of assistants and also the need to tackle this new problem which is arising because of the enormous growth of fundamentalism (much more dangerous than any other 'ism').

The practice of reading the Bible as carried out in the Base Ecclesial Communities of Latin America, has already caused a certain repercussion in all the Churches. Indeed, it is giving rise to discussions, reactions and support in many places. This was apparent in the inter-church meetings held in the 1970s, in the World Meeting of the Lutheran Church, held in Curitiba in January 1990, and in the World Meeting of the FEBIC, held in Bogotá in July 1990.

There are many other signs in other continents of an interest in the way the Bible is read in Latin America. Because of all this, it is important to begin to think seriously about the setting up of centres of research and bible study that will aim at examining the real problems that we face in our communities.

The Ecumenical Centre of Biblical Studies (CEBI), is an attempt to respond to this 'sign of the times'. Founded in 1977, it has grown and expanded rapidly. Now it is organized in most of the States of Brazil, serving an ever-increasing number of Churches. As well as that, it receives requests from various countries in Latin America, Africa and Europe for an interchange of this kind of Bible reading.[3]

3. There has been an abundant literary output at various levels, in the publishing of Bibles, commentaries, reviews and collections.The most important Bible translations in use are: Ave Maria Bible, Jerusalem Bible, Pastoral Bible, TEB Bible (ecumenical translation), Bible of the Voices, CNBB Bible, Biblical Society Bible, Bible in Today's language. There is the Latin American Commentary: 'How to read the Bible' and reviews such RIBLA, Biblical Interpretation Review of Latin America: Biblical Studies Collections include 'Your Word is Life' of the Conference of Brazilian Religious (eight volumes); SAB Collection (Biblical Animation Service) for the month of the Bible, contains popular introductions to a large number of books of the Bible; Collection, *Palavra Vida* (Word of Life) of the CEBI. The *Biblical Bibliography of Latin America* contains information about thse various works and about the majority of non-commercial Latin American biblical publications: leaflets, pamphlets, bulletins, grants

Promoting the Pastoral Biblical Apostolate and *Lectio Divina* worldwide

LUDGER FELDKÄMPER, S.V.D.

I WOULD LIKE to approach the topic biblically and experientially. Biblically: starting with the biblical story of Philip who accompanied the Ethiopian eunuch in his reading of Scripture (Acts 8:6-40); and experientially: drawing on my own experience of thirty years involvement in the biblical ministry: 10 years as Scripture professor in a school of theology and a catechetical institute as well as founder of John Paul I Biblical Centre in the Philippines; 16 years as General Secretary of the Catholic Biblical Federation, during which we started the *Dei Verbum* Biblical-Pastoral Course at Nemi, near Rome; and another four years as its coordinator in Rome.

I would like to share in a narrative way how his ministry has been – and is being – continued since the promulgation of *Dei Verbum* by many sisters and brothers around the world whose hearts have been set on fire (see Lk 24:32) with love for the word of God and who were able to bring it to others (see Lk 12,49).

OFFICIAL PROMOTION OF BIBLICAL PASTORAL MINISTRY
SINCE VATICAN II

The Dogmatic Constitution *Dei Verbum* on Divine Revelation, promulgated on November 18, 1965, in its closing paragraph expressed the hope of the Council Fathers in words which explain everything that is contained in the phrase 'promoting biblical pastoral ministry': 'In this way, therefore, through the reading and study of the sacred books "the word of God may spread rapidly and be glorified" (2 Thess 3:1)

Ludger Feldkämper svd taught Scripture in the Philippines, and served as Secretary General of the Catholic Biblical Federation (1984-2000).

and the treasure of revelation, entrusted to the Church, may more and more fill the hearts of all. Just as the life of the Church is strengthened through more frequent celebration of the Eucharistic mystery, similar we may hope for a new stimulus for the life of the Spirit from a growing reverence for the word of God, which "lasts forever" (Is 40:8; see 1 Pet 1:23-25).'

Twenty years later, an Extraordinary Synod of Bishops lamented the fact that '*Dei Verbum* had been much neglected' – a phrase which Pope John Paul II repeated in an audience to the Executive Committee of the Catholic Biblical Federation in 1986, challenging them to do something about it.

In 1993, the Pontifical Biblical Commission published with the approval of Pope John Paul II its document, 'Interpretation of Sacred Scripture in the Life of the Church', which may be considered a post-Vatican II commentary on chapters III (The Divine Inspiration and the Interpretation of Sacred Scripture) and VI (Sacred Scripture in the Life of the Church) of *Dei Verbum*. Here we find a succinct definition of 'promoting biblical-pastoral ministry': 'to make known the Bible as the Word of God and source of life' (n. 3) It also finds reason to rejoice in seeing the Bible in the hands of people of lowly condition and of the poor; they can bring to its interpretation and to its actualization a light more penetrating, from the spiritual and existential point of view, than that which comes from a learning that relies upon its own resources alone (see Mt 11:25)' (n. 3)

Pope Benedict XVI, addressing the participants of the International Congress 'Sacred Scripture in the Life of the Church on the Fortieth Anniversary of *Dei Verbum*' in Rome, September 14 to 18, 2005, spoke of a 'a new spiritual spring' in the wake of promoting 'the ancient tradition of *Lectio divina* ... as a firm point of biblical pastoral ministry.' And he chose 'The Word of God in the Life and the Mission of the Church' as the theme of the 2008 Synod of Bishops.

A BIBLICAL MODEL FOR THE BIBLICAL PASTORAL MINISTRY

Asked for a short explanation of biblical apostolate, one of the general secretaries of the Catholic Biblical Federation answered succinctly: 'Continuing where Philip left off.' He was thinking of the story of Philip and the Ethiopian (Acts 8:26-40).

Indeed, this passage of the Acts can be considered a model for both the biblical pastoral ministry and for *lectio divina*.

The Ethiopian had a text of sacred Scripture and was reading it. The first step in biblical pastoral ministry is making the Bible accessible, through translation, production and distribution – a task which the Catholic Church, after the Second Vatican Council, is doing in many countries hand in hand with the Bible Societies.

Secondly, the Ethiopian had a question, and sought Philip's help in understanding the text. The Bible, a book of a different time and different culture, containing God's word in human words, has a meaning and a message for us here and now, which may not be immediately evident. Responsible and fruitful reading of the book requires a guide.

Thirdly, starting with the passage of Scripture which the Ethiopian was reading, Philip proclaimed the Good News of Jesus. He does not stop with an explanation of the text, with exegesis; he moves on to evangelization.

Hence, the reading of Scripture on the road is shown as a process: from the book to the message of the book, which is ultimately the person of Jesus. It is a process that suggests the different steps or aspects of *lectio divina*: from reading (*lectio*) to discerning the message (*meditatio*) to an encounter of the person of Jesus (oratio) and finally to a joyous continuation of the journey (action / contemplation).

'PHILIPS' IN OUR MIDST – WOMEN AND MEN OF THE WORD

Promoting the biblical pastoral ministry means 'continuing where Philip left off.' During my years of involvement in the biblical pastoral ministry I have been able to verify the truth of this statement in encountering many 'Philips' around the world. I would like to introduce some of them. All, in one way or another, have helped others to encounter through the Scriptures the person of Jesus Christ. All of them grew into their roles of being servants of the Word for others through what might seem small experiences and the inspiration of other persons.

Carlos Mesters

In 1989, during a Latin American meeting of the Catholic Biblical Federation in Mendes, near Rio de Janeiro, Brazil, Dom Luís G.

Fernandes, a retired Brazilian Archbishop, who was referred to as the 'patriarch of the Basic Ecclesial Communities' told us that Carlos Mesters is rightly called the 'Philip of Latin America'.

Before meeting Carlos in person, I had come to know of him through his writings – which have become classics about the popular reading of the Bible – and through the 1978 Second Plenary Assembly of the World Catholic Federation for the Biblical Apostolate (later simplified to Catholic Biblical Federation) in Malta. In his keynote address the outgoing President, Cardinal König of Vienna, surprised many of those present – biblical scholars and people involved in the biblical-pastoral ministry – with the statement: 'Our task is not first and foremost to interpret a book, but to interpret life; but this we do in the light of the Word which is given to us in a privileged way in the Book.' Later the cardinal's speech-writer confided to us: 'This is from Carlos Mesters – but now it's from the Cardinal!'

Carlos has promoted the biblical apostolate worldwide also through the Catholic Biblical Federation. I gladly recall his contributions at the plenary assemblies in 1990 (Bogotá) and in 1996 (Hong Kong). In Bogotá he was the mastermind behind the Final Statement – based on Luke 24:13-35, the Risen Lord and the disciples on the road to Emmaus. In Hong Kong he led us every day in *lectio divina* on John 4 – Jesus in dialogue with the Samaritan Woman. He remarkably enriched those two assemblies; at the same time the Federation provided a 'sounding board' for Carlos.

Carlo Maria Martini

I first met Fr – and later Cardinal – Carlo Maria Martini when, as a professor at the Pontifical Biblical Institute in Rome, he taught us textual criticism. None of us students at the time had any inkling that one day he would be the great promoter of *lectio divina* and would fill the cathedral of Milan with thousands of young people, and would turn out to be the most prolific spiritual writer in Italy whose books would be translated into innumerable languages.

From him I learned the art of reading attentively. This is something everybody can do and has to do when reading the Bible. Not everybody can handle the intricacies of the historical-critical method. Nor can we expect that all Christian faithful or people in general become 'mini-exegetes' in order to have easy access to Sacred Scripture and come to the 'excelling knowledge of Jesus Christ (Phil 3:8)' (see *Dei Verbum*, nn. 22 and 25). But Bible seminars in various parts of the world have shown that all are capable of reading attentively, applying simple tools which can lead them to the joy of discovering the hidden treasures of the Word.

Cardinal Martini's greatest contribution to the biblical apostolate worldwide lies in the promotion of *lectio divina*. I would like to mention as particularly significant, a conference he gave in 1990 on the twenty-fifth anniversary of *Dei Verbum* in the crowded aula of the Gregorian University in Rome. The Cardinal took up the complaint of the Second Extraordinary Synod of Bishops in 1985 and of John Paul II in the following year, that *Dei Verbum* had been neglected. This disregard, he said, did not concern biblical scholarship, but the implementation of *Dei Verbum* 25[1] which deals with *lectio divina* even though the term was not explicitly mentioned there. One thing is sure: after this talk of his – and perhaps also because of it – *lectio divina* has at least been mentioned in almost every Vatican document that was published since.[2]

Michel de Verteuil

Fr de Verteuil is another promoter of the biblical apostolate. This book includes a convincing testimony by Ms Pat Elie on Fr Michel's way of promoting *lectio divina* as the core of the biblical pastoral ministry.[3] Reading her text, who would not think of the saying of the Lord: 'By their fruits you will know them' (Mt 7:16)?

Michel has promoted *lectio divina* not only in Trinidad. He has for many years, visited Ireland for *lectio divina* seminars. Starting in 1987, he regularly came to Nemi, Italy, as a resource person to the *Dei Verbum* Biblical-Pastoral Course. The people he introduced there to *lectio divina* were always a mixed and international group. Through him the course participants discovered *lectio divina* as the heart not only of the

---

1. Carlo M. Martini, '*Lectio Divina* – The Practice of Lectio Divina in the Biblical-Pastoral Ministry', BDV 19 (2/1991)8-13.

2. 1992 – *Pastores Dabo Vobis* (47); 1993 – *Interpretation of the Bible in the Church*;1996 – *Vita Consacrata* (6. 94. 101); 1999 – *Ecclesia in America* (31); 2001 –*Ecclesia in Oceania* (38); .2001 *Novo Millennio Ineunte* (39. 40); 2002 *Rosarium Virginis Mariae* (29); 2003 *Pastores Gregis;* 15.

3. See Pat Elie, '*Lectio Divina* in Trinidad according to the Method of Fr Michel de Verteuil', pp. 57-68, *supra*.

course, but of the biblical-pastoral ministry as well.

Asian Sisters

Now, I would like to present another group of ministers of the Word, Asian Sisters of various congregations. I came to know all of them personally at different times and in different places during my assignment in the Philippines and as General Secretary of the Catholic Biblical Federation (CBF).

I start with the Benedictine Sister Henrietta Sebastian. directress of the St Benedict Institute for the training of catechists and of the John XXIII Social Centre – located in the northern and southern parts of the Philippines, respectively. She first invited me to teach Scripture to her student catechists and then she was instrumental in getting me involved in the biblical apostolate.

It was she who advised me to change my approach to teaching: 'Always a one-man-show. Only lecture method. Very little praying! Hardly any singing!' I must have taken her constructive criticism to heart because some time later a participant in one of our courses commended the 'holistic approach' in our seminars.

It was her suggestion that we start a biblical centre After reflection, consultation, discussion and prayer the John Paul I Biblical Centre, the first regional biblical centre in the Philippines was founded in the city of Vigan, Ilocos Sur. For 26 years it has served the fourteen dioceses of Northern Luzon and has became the model for ten other regional biblical centres in the country.

She also proposed – even before she joined the staff of the centre – that we work out together an introductory course on the Bible for the simple people in the barrios (villages). Her experience in the forma-tion of catechists for pastoral work among those people contributed greatly to the Basic Bible Seminar (BBS), with what came to be called the 'Vigan method', a reading method that is based on the first three steps of *lectio divina,* moving from the text (*lectio*), which is to become a living word (*meditatio*) which solicits a response (*oratio*).[4] Over a span of 25 years, the BBS has reached far beyond the Philippines to Indonesia, Malaysia, Myanmar, Thailand, India, Hong Kong, Mainland

---

4. www.c-b-f.org, under Biblical-Pastoral Ministry, Approaches.

China, Papua New Guinea, American Samoa, Australia and Singapore; to Italy. Germany and Russia; to Zaire, Zambia, Kenya.[5]

The story of Sister Tomasa –'Tammy'– Saberon, a Filipina Columban Sister, sounds like the continuation of Sister Henrietta's. With Sisters Helen Ryan, Kathleen Geaney, and Rene O'Donoghue (all Columban sisters) she participated in one of the first Basic Bible Seminars conducted by the staff of John Paul I Biblical Centre. This may have been the beginning of the discovery of her personal vocation. She carried her commitment to the biblical apostolate with her on subsequent mission appointments. In Hong Kong she arranged to have the BBS translated into Chinese and started the biblical apostolate among Filipino domestic workers. About 120,000 in number, they make up 50% of the Catholic Church in Hong Kong.

On her next assignment – Myanmar, Burma – she started offering the Bible seminar in the local language. Her team also publishes, as follow-up material for the seminar participants, a commentary on the Sunday Gospels, Daily Bible Reading Guide and a Newsletter. And she has been appointed by the Bishops' Conference of Myanmar to the National Office for Biblical Apostolate.

Sister Emma Gunanto, an Indonesian Ursuline Sister and a professional teacher worked, 1977-1982, for the Indonesian Catholic Biblical Association on a common project with the United Bible Societies, translating the Old Testament into Today's Indonesian Version. After that, she was involved in giving retreats to lay people in a Jesuit retreat house. During these years the Word became her daily food. She also became sensitive to the plea of lay people: 'Sister, who will explain the Bible to us?'

During a 1988 sabbatical year when she participated in the *Dei Verbum* Course at Nemi, Italy, her 'heart was opened for the worldwide biblical apostolate'. Back in Indonesia in February 1989, she founded the Angela Merici Biblical Centre, and within two years, the local bishop asked her to become the chairwoman of the diocesan Commission for the Biblical Apostolate. She is fulltime involved in the biblical ministry, by teaching courses, facilitating seminars, giving talks, organizing Bible camps and writing booklets and folders.

5. John Paul I Biblical Center, BBS Silver Edition, 2006, p. 3

Since 1996 she has been Sub-regional Coordinator for Southeast Asia of the Catholic Biblical Federation which she describes as 'a worldwide community of people who have been touched by the Word, and are committed to make it known, loved and lived.'

Sister Maura Cho of the Korean Congregation of the Sisters of our Lady of Perpetual Help I consider the pioneer – or one of the pioneers – of the biblical-pastoral movement in Korea. She works in catechetics for several years. Then a serious illness led to her being hospitalized and kept in isolation. During this time Maura started to read the Bible from the beginning. Reading Genesis 1:31 – 'God saw everything God had made, and behold, it was very good' – she realized that 'The Bible is not just about creation, about Adam and Eve, about Abraham; no, it is also about me!' With this 'key' she kept on reading.

When she was finally released from the hospital, Sister Maura could not be silent about what she had heard and seen (see Acts 4:20). Soon she got her sisters excited about this way of reading the Bible. Thus the Catholic Bible Life Movement was born. The Sisters formed animators for the biblical apostolate, called Servants of the Word. They produced simple commentaries and published a biblical review. But Sister Maura went further, making radio and television programmes, and she and her Sisters and other Servants of the Word created an interactive Bible Learning Program on the internet.

Sister Maura has been actively involved in several of the international CBF meetings. During the plenary assembly of 2002 in Lebanon, she lead the Assembly in the daily *lectio divina* on passages from the Acts of the Apostles. She produced a booklet, complete with drawings from one of her Sisters, she introduced the participants into a well-received method which some have since called the Korean method of Bible sharing.

Carlos Mesters and Maura Cho were the main speakers in one of the annual residential seminars of SEDOS (the Documentation and Study Service of the Missionary Congregations in Rome). After Maura finished her talk – not about understanding the Word of God, but standing under it – the Philip of Latin America told her: 'Maura, we speak different languages, but talk about exactly the same thing!'

Sister Maria Ko Ha Fong, born in Macao, grew up in Hong Kong.

As a young Salesian Sister she was sent abroad for studies, first to Turin and Rome, then earning a doctorate in theology at the University of Münster, specializing on Scripture and Patristics. Her special area of interest is reading the Bible with Asian eyes, the topic of her keynote address during the 1996 plenary assembly of the CBF. She helps guide us in the Catholic Biblical Federation to become more and more sensitive to reading the Bible 'in context'.

Laypeople

Hong Kong is the home also of Ms Cecilia Chui, a young Chinese laywoman, a professional in public relations, with a Master's degree this field from an Australian university.

She participated in the first Chinese Basic Bible Seminar (BBS), organized by the Hong Kong Catholic Biblical Association (HKCBA) in 1984 at the initiative of Sister Tomasa Saberon. This marked the beginning of her acquaintance with the Catholic Biblical Federation (CBF). She writes: 'Through BBS, I have learnt to take the Bible as my prayer book and the light of my life.'

Reflecting on her involvement in CBF, she said: 'I have been applying communications principles and skills to promote CBF and the biblical pastoral ministry. This interaction between my work life and biblical service enables me to see, hear, touch and taste that "the Word of God is truly alive and active" (Heb 4:12).... Through the efforts of CBF, the Bible, as a witness of faith and expression of God's message, has been enjoying growing interest in many countries. This trend has visibly contributed to greater involvement of lay people in biblical pastoral ministry.'

Mr Charles Javier has served for many years as Principal of the Elementary Department of one of the Catholic Colleges in the Province of Abra, Northern Philippines and is now the Director of one of the Catholic High Schools in the provincial capital. A superb teacher and able administrator he is musically gifted. At our monthly Bible days, whenever he would remember a song related to what we were dealing with, he would give me a sign. I would stop lecturing and he would teach the song and / or would lead the group in the singing. This not only made for variety; it also created a joyful and relaxed atmosphere. Moreover, through those songs the lesson would be remembered much better.

During a Youth Gospel Festival we invited school classes and youth organizations to bring along a song they had composed. To help them, we distributed an A4-size sheet with a short article – from the Lumko Institute of South Africa – entitled: 'How to Compose a Gospel Song'. The more than 900 participants brought along no fewer than 50 songs! After this experience, we organized a one-week Gospel Song Workshop. Twenty young people took up the challenge to compose, under our guidance and supervision, a song based on a Sunday Gospel of Cycle B (St Mark). This project was extended later to the other lectionary cycles. The songs produced in this way could be used in Bible seminars, for catechesis, in the liturgy; the could be broadcast over the local and diocesan radios.

Increasingly, lay people are coming forward with professional training in Scripture. One I would mention is Dr Daniel Kosch, a Swiss lay theologian.

As a trained exegete, involved at parish level in Bible reading in groups or small communities, he later served the biblical pastoral ministry at national level as director of the central office of the Swiss Catholic Biblical Association (Schweizer Katholisches Bibelwerk – SKB), an association founded in 1935. As director he represented SKB in the Catholic Biblical Federation.

He contributed significantly to the Biblical-Pastoral Meeting of European Bishops in Freising, Germany, in February 1994 on 'Holy Scripture in the Life of the Churches in Europe now and in the time ahead', organized by CCEE (the Council of European Bishops´ Conferences) and CBF. At the Fifth Plenary Assembly of the Federation in Hong Kong, he delivered one of the main papers on 'The Wealth of the Bible and the Diversity of Readings – A Methodological Reflection' He acknowledged his indebtedness to Carlos Mesters whose 'manner of reflecting on and clarifying praxis' had stamped biblical-pastoral work in Switzerland in recent years and had helped to give clear structure to his own thoughts.

From 1996-2001 Daniel Kosch was the first lay person to be Moderator of the CBF, untll he was called to another leadership post in the Church in Switzerland.

Divine Word Missionaries

While reflecting on 'Promoting Biblical Pastoral Ministry worldwide' I may be allowed to mention also some 'Philips' in my own international missionary congregation.

St Arnold Janssen gave the name Society of the Divine Word to the society he founded. In explaining it, he referred to the Word of the Father, the Son of God; to the Word of the Son, the preaching of the Gospel in the Church; and to the Word of the Holy Spirit, the inspired Scriptures. Since the proclamation of the Dogmatic Constitution *Dei Verbum* it has been recognized more and more that the biblical apostolate is and should be an integral part or 'characteristic dimensions' of our missionary activities.

The outstanding promoter of this insight has been Superior General Fr Henry Heekeren who had been trained in Scripture at the Pontifical Biblical Institute and who had taught Scripture and given biblical retreats on all continents. As the 'Philip' of the entire SVD, he inspired many confreres with love for the Word of God who turned out to be Philips themselves – each bringing to this ministry their own gifts and skills.

When I was a novice 50 years ago, a classmate of Fr. Heekeren, Carlos Pape from Chile, told me, 'If you want to develop a love for Scripture, it has to come now, in the novitiate. In theology they will do everything to destroy it!' After his ordination, back in his home country, Carlos' own love of Scripture brought him to closely work together with Fr Bernard Hurault, the 'author' of the 'Biblia Latino-Americana' and in 1973 he published a New Testament which had a first edition of 500.000 copies.

Brazilian Fr Edenio Valle had the idea of a Bible-reading program for all religious of Latin America in connection with the celebration of the 500 years of evangelization of that continent. He got Carlos Mesters and others excited about this plan, which resulted in the *Palabra-Vida* ('Word-Life') Project.

An outstanding promoter of the biblical apostolate, a disciple of Carlos and walking in the footsteps of Edenio, is Fr Tom Hughes from Dublin, who has been working in Brazil for more than 30 years. At present he inspires and coordinates the biblical pastoral ministry of confreres in all SVD provinces of all North and South America. Of late, he has preached biblical retreats in other parts of the world – Philippines, Papua New Guinea, perhaps also Africa.

On the African continent Divine Word missionaries have been referred to as the 'Missionaries with the Bible.' The publishing house Verbum Bible originated in Kinshasa, Congo, and has its francophone branch there. Filipino confrere Xene Sanchez, as a student of theology came to know the Basic Bible Seminar of the John Paul I Biblical Centre. Assigned to the Republic of Congo as a missionary, he had the BBS translated first into French, then into the local languages Lingala and Kikongo. Soon it became a valuable tool for the biblical apostolate of the biblical centres in Bandundu and in Kinshasa. From there it became known in other African countries like Zimbabwe and was translated into the respective local languages.

Jean Ikanga, a young Congolese confrere, relates the discovery of his vocation to participating in a Basic Bible Seminar. On joining the Society, studying philosophy in Kinshasa, he came to know the Bible group formed by Fr Xene Sanchez. In that group, he saw how 'people were happy to devour the word of God. He invited us to attend and to see what was going on and to appreciate the experience.'

Studying theology in the biblical department at Tangaza College, Nairobi, Kenya, he and a fellow seminarian from Kenya soon they found out that the people of their Bible group in a slum parish had different needs in approaching the Bible. 'If the academic understanding was a quest for me in the university, it was not the same for them. With a listening heart, I realized that a reading of the Bible for life or in order to read and pray for daily life was their need...I started then to read both their life and the Bible.'

Back in Kinshasa for his pastoral year, together with the Indian confrere, Fr Mathew Thekkeyil, the director of the new Biblical Centre Liloba, he went to many parishes of Kinshasa to give the BBS. He recalls the passionate testimony of a man from Rwanda during a Bible sharing on forgiveness: '"This text is a great challenge to me as a refugee here in Kenya without family. My wife was killed after being raped. This text calls me to forgive the killers of my wife. How can I forgive them if I know the hurt, anger I have is because of them"'. He shed tears and paused for a while and said: '"This passage of the Bible is very strong to me…"'

After such experiences, Jean, with the help of two Kenyan confreres, decided to translate the BBS manual into Kiswahili, adapting it at the same time to local conditions. 'Many Christians saw that, like the Muslims do with the Koran, it would be better to give an initial thirst of the Bible to their children. Thus, a three-hour BBS for children was drafted..'

After many Basic Bible Seminars in Kenya, he went to Tanzania. There people told him: 'It is no more the priest, the bishop or a friend, ignorant of my life and situation, who speak to me, but it is God who knows me individually who speaks to me. The Bible is now the book of my life (*kitabu cha maisha yangu*).'

When Jean was studying in Nairobi and translating the Basic Bible Seminar, Fr Tom Leyden from Ballinrobe, Co. Mayo, was the spiritual director in the SVD Common Formation Centre. He has committed himself to reading the entire Bible four times each year, and he intends to do that till death.

He tells a story of how in a densely crowded and noisy side street in Nairobi, he came across a man sitting on the ground with an outstretched hand, palm downwards. The man was blind and his fingers were reading Braille in his open book. When Tom asked him in Kiswahili what he was reading, he said he was reading the Bible. The text was John chapter 17.

The Catholic Biblical Federation

In presenting these 'Philips', time and again I had to make cross references to other 'Philips'. Their collaboration has taken place within, and has been made possible through the Catholic Biblical Federation. To answer a question about the nature and purpose of the Federation, it would be sufficient to repeat: 'To continue where Philip left of.'

Many outstanding Philips who operated within the frame of the Federation – like Cardinal Augustine Bea, whom we consider to be its founder and Bishop Alberto Ablondi who as President guided and inspired the Federation for 12 years – would deserve a detailed presentation. I will limit myself to relating how people who have had first-hand acquaintance with the Federation, see it and try to encapsulate it in a symbol.

For Fr Gabriel Naranjo Salazar, C.M. (Colombia), the CBF is its members and is a corner of faith, and he points out: 'In it I have found a space to express and nourish my faith, both human and Catholic (but not in the confessional sense)'.

The image offered by Bishop Arturo Bastes, S.V.D. (Philippines) is of a dynamo.

For Grace Celia (Malta), the CBF 'is a positive ray of hope that kept growing (and now it seems to be going from strength to strength) after Vatican II, working for the Word of God in response to the Council's call to make the Word more accessible to the people.'

Sister Maura Cho, SOLPH (Korea / USA) 'would like to view the CBF as a bridge on which so many people of the Bible in our days have communicated.'

Dr Daniel Kosch (Switzerland) points out that 'lay people, religious men and women, priests, bishops, people of different cultures, nationalities and languages, representatives of diverse spiritualities and theological traditions – all of these have formed and are forming the life of the CBF. Thus the Federation has become a mirror of the Bible with its 72 books, its countless and most diverse characters und stories, with the great lines of hope in redemption through Jesus Christ, of trust into the one God, and of love for the poor and abandoned, but also with its exciting variety of sundry experiences of world and of life'.

In the mind of Fr Abraham Mariaselvam (India) 'the CBF may be described as the heart that beats for the service of the Word of God.'

Rev. A. Miller Milloy, General Secretary of UBS (Great Britain), see the CBF is 'the advocate of the Bible cause in the Catholic Church'.

Fr Paul Puthanangady, S.D.B. (India) descibes the CBF as 'an instrument of the Spirit of Christ in the emerging new era for building up a community of love around the Word of Love of the Father, going beyond all religious and other groupings'.

We may leave the last word to Fr James Swetnam, S.J. (Rome): 'I associate with CBF a much needed and quite important movement of the Church, mandated by Vatican II, to promote the pastoral use of the Bible in the Church. Personally, work in this area, especially with *lectio divina* but also with homiletics, has helped me get a better

understanding of the work of the professional exegete in the interpretation of Scripture.'

CONCLUSION

There is reason to rejoice in the many 'Philips' who have placed
their various personal talents, professional skills and wealth of experience at the service of the Word, many of them within the structure
and framework of the Catholic Biblical Federation.

One can only hope and pray that through the courses and other
services of the newly founded Dominican Biblical Center and through
many 'Philips' trained by it the Word will spread and be received with
honor. (*Dei Verbum*, n. 26).

Lectio Divina and the Story of the Widow

✠ LUCIANO MONARI

IN A BEAUTIFUL book entitled *Practice of Biblical Text,* Cardinal C. M. Martini collected some examples of *lectio divina* to teach this approach to the biblical text – an approach, the cardinal says, that every Christian boy and girl should learn to practise, at least from the age of twelve. The introductory chapter presents the aim of the author: to find an effective answer to the question: How may I use the biblical text for a meditation that flows into prayer and blossoms in actual deeds in life? And he explains: 'Prayer aims at changing the heart, aims at conversion. And I confess: that is the question I've been trying to answer all my life long, an answer which has always to be renewed, tested, launched again, worked out again.'

Cardinal Martini imagines building a bridge which allows the difficult passage from the biblical text to life: a bridge with eight arches described in eight Latin words: *lectio, meditatio, contemplatio, oratio, consolatio, discretio, deliberatio, actio.* These words taken together draw a real itinerary from text to life – like a process of incarnation of the Word of God in human life. In this spirit, I'll try, as I can, to walk this road, starting from a text Mk 12:38-44.

THE TEXT
As he [Jesus] taught, he said: Beware of the scribes, who like to walk around in long robes, and to be greeted with respect in the market-places, and to have the best seats in the synagogues and places of honour at banquets! They devour widows' houses and for the sake of appearance say long prayers. They will receive the

✠ Luciano Monari, a Vice-President of the Italian Bishops' Conference, has spoken on Scripture at the last three World Youth Assemblies. He studied under Cardinal Martini, and was invited to the Limerick conference on Cardinal Martini's recommendation.

greater condemnation.

He sat down opposite the treasury, and watched the crowd putting money into the treasury. Many rich people put in large sums. A poor widow came and put in two small copper coins, which are worth a penny. Then he called his disciples and said to them: Truly I tell you, this poor widow has put in more than all those who are contributing to the treasury. For all of them have contributed out of their abundance; but she out of her poverty has put in everything she had, all she had to live on.

LECTIO

The first step *lectio*, wants to answer the question: what does this text teach? What is its literal meaning? It's a necessary step because the letter (the literal meaning) is the only solid base upon which every other meaning must stand – if we don't want to fall into arbitrariness.

It's not difficult to grasp the basic structure. It is a proper diptych, a unity composed of two pictures, different but tied together so that they give light one to the other and interpret one another, both through their similarities and through their differences.

The first picture is a warning Jesus directs to the crowd, taking its starting point from the behaviour of the scribes (vv. 38-40); the second is a teaching addressed to the disciples, a teaching suggested by observing a poor widow (vv. 41-44).

So: the scribes – a widow; the official scholars of Mosaic law who receive great honour in Judaic religious society – a woman who is characterised only by her social weakness. The text compares and contrasts these two figures; let's see how.

The first picture is, as we said, a warning of Jesus to the crowd, given by Jesus as a teacher ('as he taught, he said...'): 'Beware of...' The teaching supposes that the crowd could be deceived by appearances and needs to be told that the reality is different from what it seems to be and that they must beware, then.

Let's look at the scribes. They are scholars expert in Jewish law. Every law needs a correct interpretation so that all its requirements may be shown clearly, all the possibilities explored, all the doubts overcome. The scribes devote their lives to this study, examining the text, collect-

ing the interpretations in the tradition. They can teach with authority the real meaning of every word and of every element in the Law.
Normally, they belong to the sect of Pharisees who are representatives
of a fervent religious spirit which generously assumes the obligations
deriving from the law; they indeed try to reach a perfect obedience
to the law through additional deeds, not strictly commanded by the
law, and exceeding the letter of the law itself. Jesus draws a picture of
them with five lines.

They 'like to walk around in long robes'. This trait may be explained
in many ways but the basic meaning is clear enough: They love to wear
showy dresses, to be seen, to be admired by people.

They 'like to be greeted with respect in the market-places, and to
have the best seats in the synagogues and places of honour at banquets.' Three similar traits which express the scribes' desire to be atop
in society. They are – or ought to be – servants of God's law; but they
use this service to gain respect in society.

We find then a specifically religious trait: 'for the sake of appearance they say long prayers.' That means: they really say long prayers,
but their aim in praying is not to give glory to God but to gain glory
for themselves: to be seen, admired, esteemed by the people. The
fact that this is a religious trait (the prayer) makes this behaving even
more reproachful because it shows a hypocritical religiosity which
presumes to be addressed to God but in fact is looking for a worldly
gain (admiration, social success).

Together with all these traits there is another, one that is puzzling:
they 'devour widows' houses.' How do the scribes do this? Perhaps
through their legal interpretations? Or asking too high a price for their
legal counsels? Perhaps... We don't know exactly and the interpreters
offer different explanations. But it's not a problem. Some things are
clear: first of all these scribes look for economical gains just as they
look for social acknowledgements; secondly, they don't refrain from
damaging persons like widows who are poor and weak, socially and
economically; thirdly, they are greedy and unjust while they are per-
forming their religious duties.

So far the picture. Now, what to think of a behaviour like that?
Jesus answers: 'They will receive the greater condemnation.' You

will understand: 'from God'. They may receive glory from men, but they will suffer a harsh judgement from God. Their behaviour has to be condemned and to receive a greater condemnation because it accompanies a religious way of life. Religious membership increases reproachfulness (and deserves a *greater* condemnation) just because the behaviour involves 'using God' to acquire worldly gains and because it can't hide under the justification of an uninformed conscience.

It would be easy to find in the prophetic books similar accusations against a nasty use of religion: Is 1:10-17; Jer 7; Amos 5:21-27…

The second picture is more complex and has two moments. The first is the observation of alms-giving people in the temple (vv. 41-42); the second is the interpretation of the scene (vv. 43-44).

First, we look at the actors: Jesus sitting before the building of the treasury where money is kept; the crowd which passes putting money into the treasury; a part of the crowd (the rich ones) is regarded with particular attention and one notes that the alms are huge; another part of the crowd is observed (notably a widow) and one notes that she offers two little coins, a penny-worth. The text underlines the contrast between the quantity of money offered by the rich and the few, little coins offered by the widow.

The second part of the picture shows Jesus calling his disciples to himself and giving them a teaching which reverses the appearances. The rich people seem to have offered much and the poor widow less; in fact the widow's offering is much greater than that of the rich. Why?

One must pass from a quantitative consideration of the alms (the economic value of the offerings) to a qualitative consideration (the existential meaning of the offerings). Changing the observation point, we see that the rich ones appear to be offering extra money, which is not necessary for their survival (something which does not affect directly their existence); the widow, on the contrary, is offering from what is necessary to her; the offering affects her own life. One could say: the rich ones offered something they had (money); the widow (in the two coins) offered herself, something of her life itself.

We can connect this scene with the greatest commandment of the law, the text we find together with the Shemà: 'You shall love the Lord your God with all your heart, and with all your soul, and with all your might.' That's exactly what the widow did, unlike the scribes' behaviour. The widow proves to be an extraordinary example of obedience to the first and basic commandment of the Law.[1]

We'll add another remark: our text belongs to a series of episodes located in Jerusalem, in the Temple; these episodes, from the point of view of their form, are controversies between Jesus and the Jews. We are not at school trying to utter abstract judgements on impersonal behaviours, as if from the outside; the text opposes Jesus' religion and the scribes' religion and asks the hearers to side with Jesus. The widow, with her tiny but great alms, gives an opportunity for Jesus to express his way of understanding religion, man's relation to God.

So far, the text seems to be perfectly clear; it doesn't present particular problems of interpretation. Perhaps the sole interesting explanation would be to cite other parallel texts which may help to give our text amplitude and depth. I underline only one macroscopic dynamic aspect of our text: before Jesus, the herald of the Kingdom of God and prophet, two religious figures are put, one against the other: the scribes and a widow. Every reader should start with a pre-judgement: acknowledgement of the religious superiority of the scribes: they know the Law in all its parts, all its interpretations while the poor widow (we must presume) doesn't; they express socially a dominant religious interest, while the widow doesn't. In the eyes of the religious society of that time, and in our eyes too, the scribes are the model of religious life; in the eyes of the eschatological prophet, on the contrary, the real model is the widow. The hearers are asked to pass from their 'natural' judgement to a new judgement which depends on Jesus' revelation, on his new way of seeing deeply and expressing God' ultimate judgement on man's behaviour.

MEDIATIO

This second step tries to answer the question: what does the text say to us? Which are the values we can find in the text?

First of all, we see a negative value: to seek others' admiration with our behaviour. Social recognition is a desirable good. But when it is

---

1. It is interesting to remember that Maimonides interprets the expression: 'with all your might' with the meaning of: 'with all your possessions, with all your richness.' Exactly what the widow does.

sought too eagerly and becomes the motive of behaviour and choices, it turns into a negative value because it urges people to make some choices not because they are good and just, but because they are profitable. We regress to an infantile morality which hasn't yet developed an authentic perception of good. The fact that a similar behaviour can go together with an evident lack of sensibility towards people who are socially weak (they devour widows' houses) is the proof that we are in the presence of an undeveloped morality.

This aspect becomes even more evident if we take into account the religious experience ('for the sake of appearance they say long prayers'). Their religious practices are not for the sake of God, to proclaim his glory, but for the sake of appearance to acquire glory, to receive a worldly credit. A real religious attitude requires transparency which means: not to have double ends, but to seek sincerely what our deeds, our choices express. And, particularly, to live it 'before God' and not 'before the world'; to seek 'to please the Lord' and not the world; to search for God's approval and not the world's. 'I am God Almighty – God says to Abraham – walk before me and be blameless.' (Gen 17:1) And Jesus in Matthew's Gospel: 'Beware of practising your piety before others in order to be seen by them, for then you have no reward from your Father in heaven.' (Mt 6:1ff)

I could also cite a series of Pauline texts where the apostle reveals his attitude and the source of his detachment; 'We refuse to practise cunning or to falsify God's word ... we commend ourselves to the conscience of everyone in the sight of God.' (2 Cor 4:2; see 1Thess 2:4).

In the widow, on the contrary, are shown the highest values of religion. First of all, total dedication to God. As we have already pointed out, God must be loved 'with all the heart, with all the soul...' That little word, *all*, is decisive; if God is God, one cannot measure what to give him; the only measure suitable to him is all, the totality. That's why the widow is an example for every disciple. This radical, total love is required in the Gospel not only towards God, but even towards Jesus as God's revelation. The disciple who wants to follow him must 'give up all his possessions.' For this reason, when Jesus is going to explain the widow's act he calls his disciples; the teaching is particularly for them.

This fullness in the gift has its roots in a parallel fullness in trust, in faith. One can give all to God if one trusts in God without reservation because one is convinced that God is Father and will not let his sons and daughters miss anything necessary. Here, too, we find many parallel texts: Mt 6:25ff, for example: 'Therefore, I tell you, do not worry about your life, what you will eat or what you will drink, or about your body, what you will wear... For it is the Gentiles who strive for all these things; and indeed your heavenly Father knows that you need all these things.' Only a deep trust in God can explain the widow's generosity.

And, finally, let's note that religion is always the offer of oneself to God. One can offer to God everything: a sheep, bread, a sacrifice, a prayer, a vow. But anyhow one must offer oneself, one's life, one's freedom, one's hopes. 'I appeal to you therefore, brothers and sisters, by the mercy of God, to present your bodies as a living sacrifice, holy and acceptable to God, which is your spiritual worship.' (Rom 12:1) Throwing her two coins into the treasure, the widow not only gave a gift of a precise economic value; she offered God an unreserved trust, a passionate love, a solid hope.

CONTEMPLATIO

This third step, is the most delicate, a passage, Cardinal Martini says, from human activity to letting oneself be moved and led by God's grace. So far, we proceeded using literary analysis, semantic investigations, confrontations, reflections. From the start we needed to be attracted by the Lord, but we could walk on our feet with our knowledge, memory, insight, interpretative tradition, commentaries. Now we must rest for a little, calm down, soothe our desires and leave a greater room to God's activity and grace. So it becomes difficult to give precise instructions and we must draw the inner walk of the soul from outside. How?

I too am in the Temple, among these crowds who are listening to Jesus, in the group of disciples whom Jesus takes aside and teaches; and Jesus' words are directed to me. These words don't only teach a truth to be understood; they call us to participate in the religious horizon of Jesus. The pure eyes of God see the real state of being without altering it. Our eyes, however, are often made sombre by fears or by desires. I look then to the scribes, I see their eagerness to be admired,

I recognise the emptiness, the vacuity of this feeling and, slowly, step by step, the seductive desire of being admired ebbs away; the heart doesn't yearn any more for public success or approval.

On the contrary, the scene of the widow attracts me. Poor, socially powerless, religiously despicable; and what a depth of faith there is in that act of giving two coins! What inner freedom from fear! That little woman overcame all the threats connected with uncertainty of the future; she is free from the seductions of social acknowledgements.

A contemplative look approaches the woman with affection and desires to internalise the human and religious values present in her behaviour.

Now, the meaning of this text is clear: I look at the scene with Jesus' eyes and I allow to arise in my heart right feelings of attraction or of repulsion; feelings which are born from participating in the religious outlook of Jesus. In this way, step by step, my mental habits, my ego-ist ideas fade away; new images are formed, new feelings arise, new judgements, new desires. All this presupposes the reflection and the judgement we formed through the *lectio* and the *meditatio*. But the doctrinal and moral judgement, the intellectual ideas must turn into a deep motion of the heart. And the contemplation moves towards this end: not to enrich our knowledge with new ideas or new judgements, but to enrich our heart with new and deeper feelings, new and stronger beliefs.

ORATIO

Now prayer can spring forth: 'You are right, O Lord. It's not important or useful to wear rich vestments or occupy seats of prestige. Showy clothing doesn't better the quality of the heart, and social position doesn't give real greatness to those who keep it. It's the person who can lend value to the clothing and make honourable the seats, not the opposite. How many times, Lord, do I find in myself the desires of the sons of Zebedee: to sit at your right hand or your left hand, to occupy seats of honour which make my presence seem important in the eyes of the world? But I know that you are right, that ambition and career don't make me better; on the contrary I risk becoming arrogant and falling into the stupid contest of seeming, of appearing.

'Grant me, Lord, not to be trapped by outward appearances, by presumption of power, by bondage of worldly gain. I'd like that my religious life would be ruled by your way of seeing, could participate in your judgements. Above all, my Lord, make me free from searching for my gain through religious acts: may I recognise my hypocrisy when I make use of my priestly identity, and of the faith I profess for egoistic gains. May I recognise it, O Lord, and may I withdraw soon with horror. Give me a painful and live perception of your judgement, so that I'll not be surprised by a graver sentence.

'Give me, instead, the joy of giving you all: All I have and possess, you gave me – liberty, memory, intelligence, everything – all comes from you: May I give it back to you, put it into your hands, without reserve, without fear. I believe in you, Lord; I believe in your love and I would succeed in trusting in you, always. If you take care of the lilies of the field, of the birds of the air, you'll take care of me too, and with a greater care. So, why do I fear? Why does uncertainty for the future upset my thoughts and paralyse my capacity to give and to love?

'I'd like, my Lord, to reach the inner freedom of the widow; to be able to put into your hands all I have, the little I have, with a whole trust, with certainty that I'll lose nothing and I'll gain all.

'"I am continually with you; you hold my right hand. You guide me with your counsel and afterwards you'll receive me with honour… for me it is good to be near God; I have made the Lord God my refuge, to tell of all your works".'

CONSOLATIO

Consolation is the fifth step. The biblical texts may free us from fears which block us and make us sad, and may renew in us the joy and the deep desire for God, and for his gifts. So we read in Paul's Letter to the Romans: 'Whatever was written in former days was written for our instruction, so that by steadfastness and by the encouragement of the scriptures we might have hope.' (Rom 15:4) What do we mean by the word 'consolation'? Not only a psychological relief of sufferings, but, more, the strength not to be crushed by them, to be able to renew hope in every situation. In Paul's words: 'We are afflicted in every way, but not crushed, perplexed, but not driven to despair, persecuted but not forsaken; struck down but not destroyed; always carrying in the body the death of Jesus, so that the life of Jesus may also made visible in our bodies.' (2 Cor 4:8-10)

Paradoxically, the image of the scribes may be a source of consolation. It is consolation even if I am compelled to see myself reflected in their behaviour with shame, in their desire to be honoured and in their eagerness of social acknowledgements. In fact, Jesus starts saying: 'Beware of…'. His warning is meaningful only if it is really possible to avoid a deadly danger.

Consolation means, in this case, the strength of conversion. As long as I look at myself in a mirror, as long as I make my desires the measure of my behaviour, it will be difficult for me to acknowledge my superficiality and overcome my egoism. But if I stay before the word of God, if I let myself be accused by it, then sadness for my sin turns into hope of a new life and a deep consolation blossoms in me. Worldly grief, writes saint Paul, produces death because it's a grief without hope; but godly grief produces a repentance that leads to salvation and brings no regret (see 2 Cor 7:10). Remembering the joyous event of the Corinthians' conversion, the apostle speaks admiringly: 'what earnestness, what eagerness to clear yourselves, what indignation, what alarm, what longing, what zeal, what punishment!' Look: earnestness, eagerness, indignation, alarm, longing, zeal… an extraordinary list of feelings which arise from listening to Paul's gospel. Fixing our attention on the scribes, even if their example is negative, even if we must confess on our part a similar sin, may open a road to salvation. Feelings may arise, which open the way to conversion and are a source of consolation

An even greater consolation is offered by the image of the widow. It's wonderful that there are people like her. It's wonderful that religion may not always involve mean behaviour – disguised business, like Satan insinuates in the prologue of the book of Job – but opens to the generosity of a present without limits. Admiring this poor widow, we begin anew to trust in human beings' good feelings, in our mysterious capacities for trust and love. It's true that we have an impulse to self-defence; and from this come feelings of fear, of mistrust and egoistic desires. But it's also true that our hearts are able, with God's grace, to overcome these feelings in giving ourselves. And when this succeeds we behold a marvel which reconciles us with life, with what it is to be human, with human history so full of sufferance, but so rich in courage. The consolation comes from here: not in a superficial sensation of well-being, but in a mode of hope which affects our desires.

DISCRETIO

The sixth step may be called discernment, and by it we mean that process through which we learn to acknowledge the actual motives which are at the origin of our desires and behaviours and to assess them according to their real quality – good or bad, authentic or false. Here we are helped by the Letter to the Hebrews which writes: 'Indeed, the word of God is living and active, sharper than any two-edged sword, piercing until it divides soul from spirit, joints from marrow; it is able to judge the thoughts and intentions of the heart. And before him no creature is hidden, but all are naked and laid bare to the eyes of the one to whom we must render an account.' (Heb 4:12-13)

The meaning is clear: through listening to the word of God we are put under God's gaze; and under God's gaze feelings and thoughts of our heart are separated and weighted so that each feeling, each inner impulse shows its true value: 'The heart is devious above all else' – is Jeremiah's teaching – 'it is perverse; who can understand it? I, the Lord, test the mind and search the heart.' (Jer 17:9)

What matters is no longer to work over the biblical text for its interpretation; here we must work over the interpretation of our heart, starting from the light the text is throwing upon us. From our heart desires and aspirations spring; it's from these desires that life's energy moves.

In order that we can reach a sufficient maturity and in order that our religious experience may become authentic, it's decisive to learn to discern our feelings and to recognise their origin – if they come from egoism, envy, resentment, or if, on the contrary, they bear the form of love, meekness, giving up of ourselves. The aim is not to censure every egoistic feeling (it wouldn't be useful) but to acknowledge them for what they are so as to purify them.

Listen to your heart, search in it deeply. Don't you find it too attached to the desire of appearing? Don't you think that it looks for seats of honour with too much desire? 'But I don't seek them for my sake' – your heart will say – 'I seek them for the sake of justice and for a common good.' May be; it's exactly here that your discernment becomes serious. But one must judge without hypocrisy. If you are too preoccupied with the first seats and less with the first seats which are due to others; if you love what makes you appear in a good light while you look with unease at what makes others appear in a good light, this means that in your feelings there is something incorrect, something false. There's nothing unusual in this – the contrary would be strange. But 'don't be boastful and false to the truth' – James warns us – 'such wisdom doesn't come from above; but is earthy, unspiritual, devilish' (Jas 3:14-15). Confess your feelings and start the long, slow, and some-times painful walk which can take you towards a more sincere humility.

And don't boast of what you give the Lord: you've not yet reached that widow's generosity. The true measure of generosity is not what one gives, but what one retains for oneself in giving. And you keep much – in money, acknowledgements, satisfactions. You are yet a sim-ple apprentice in the way of love: confess it with sincerity and foster in yourself the desire for conversion.

DELIBERATIO

The seventh, deliberation, is a decisive step. The aim of the *lectio divina* is not to give some grateful emotion, but to transform life according to the word of God, And decision is the decisive step. I've become a bit more aware of what I am, of what I do, of the motives which are at the origin of my deeds. Now I must decide on a new start.

Psalm 15 may be a help; in it we find the conditions for entering into the Temple of God and so into the sphere of divine life. Or I may use Psalm 101 which numbers the wise decisions of a prince: 'I will study the way that is blameless... I will walk with integrity of heart...'; afterwards, we'll make some firm resolution. It's interesting to note that this Psalm begins with praise: 'I will sing of loyalty and of justice; to you, Lord, I will sing'. *Deliberatio* is not the long list of purposes of a good will; it is, first of all, praise to God's love and justice, to God's action in man's life. From this praise, the strength of *deliberatio* arises. Of course deliberation in itself wouldn't be difficult. Who among us doesn't know the steps we ought to take towards conversion? Towards a greater conformity to God's will? The real problem is not understanding but doing what we know has to be done. We need to find and use the necessary moral strength if we don't want that deliberation to remain a mere wish. And this comes from God's grace.

ACTIO

So we've arrived at the end of our itinerary: the *actio*, the action. The word must be understood in its widest meaning. Not necessarily, 'to do something', but to change something in one's way of living (in one's feelings, ways of seeing and understanding, of judging, scale of values and so on). From the point of view of the person, it's the end of the whole process of knowledge, of decision. Human thought aims at this end, human responsibility aims at it, liberty finds here its fullness. One could say that action is the highest expression of the person because it assumes and perfects all the other moments of his/her experience.

One could recall the conclusion of Jesus' Sermon on the Mount: 'Not everyone who says to me: Lord, Lord, will enter the kingdom of heaven, but only he who does the will of my Father in heaven... Everyone then who hears these words of mine and acts on them will be like a wise man who built his house on rock.' (Mt 7:21.24)

Nor would it be right to oppose Pauline theology to Matthew because Paul too is clear about this point: God's right judgement is manifested in this, that he 'will repay according to each one's deeds.' (Rom 2:6) And we also find Paul saying: 'All of us must appear before the judgement seat of Christ, so that each may receive recompense for what has been done in the body, whether good or evil.' (2 Cor 5:10).

It is not difficult to understand what kind of changes a *lectio divina* on Mk 12 may ask and urge: a transformation in the way of living our relationships with others (not desiring to make an exhibition of ourselves, of our powers...), in the way of living religion (in a authentic fashion, before the Lord, under his gaze), in devoting ourselves to the Lord (love with all our heart). We are called to pass from a pharisaic way of life, like that of the scribes, to a style similar to that of the widow. The Gospel reaches us while we are deep in the first condition of inauthenticity and takes us step by step towards the opposite condition of authenticity. To get to this end our whole person is involved: our eyes which read, our intelligence which tries to understand, our feelings which learn to desire, our freedom which decides and now the whole of our being which shows itself in new behaviour.

Lectio Divina and the Reformed Tradition

J. CECIL McCULLOUGH

I WOULD like to thank the organizers of the conference for their invitation and to express my delight that the conference has generated so much interest. I have thoroughly enjoyed the conference and I would, therefore, like to give a small response from my own Church perspective to the whole process of *lectio divina* that has been so well described and analyzed in the conference and now so wonderfully illustrated by Bishop Monari.

My background is as follows: I am a Presbyterian minister, involved in the first seven years of my ministry in parish ministry and then in the last 35 years in the formation of students for the ministry in Beirut, Lebanon, then in New Zealand and finally in the past 20 years in Belfast. As you know, Presbyterians have a long and proud history of Bible study. They have been meeting in groups to study the Bible and to pray for several centuries; personal Bible study has been promoted as a way of spiritual development, and several societies for the promotion of personal Bible study have a long and very respected history. We also have a long tradition of Biblical preaching, so it was with great interest that I came to see what is done in our sister Church.

I have come here as a student to learn from brothers and sisters in Christ who belong to a different tradition from mine. I had heard Cardinal Martini talk in Dundalk about *lectio divina* on one of his visits to Ireland and was intrigued to find out more about it and so eagerly took up the invitation, not because I could contribute anything but because I could learn and perhaps learn something to pass on to my students and through them to my Church.

J. Cecil McCullough is a former teacher of Scripture in Beirut, professor emeritus of Queen's University, Belfast, and former editor of *Irish Biblical Studies*.

Throughout our history we have had, in the seminaries at least, two burning questions: how can we understand a text written 2000 years ago in a language no longer spoken today, to a people of very different cultures, social circumstances, religious background and even education; and then how can we make that book relevant to people of our present day. In the middle of that, particularly in the first half of the twentieth century came the question, how can we or should we use the findings of historical criticism in that quest, bearing in mind that there are changing fashions in modern biblical criticism as there are in everything else and that today's assured truth might be tomorrow's laughing stock.

So the challenge I face is how, in this age, can I prepare students for the ministry or priesthood to preach from the Bible in a way which will deepen their own faith and that of the listeners and at the same time take account of modern critical scholarship at the point it is at. How does one reconcile the pulpit and the New Testament guild? I was fascinated to see that this was an underlying theme of the conference here.

FOUR APPROACHES

In my tradition I have observed several approaches to this.

Many ignore the critical approach and will have nothing to do with it. Occasionally, I would find a student who puts his or her pen down noisily the moment you mention the Historical Jesus or the authorship of Ephesians. In fact, in our tradition, when a young person is called to come to theological college to train to be a minister, you will often find well-meaning gentlemen or ladies who approach the student for the ministry to warn them strongly against the teaching which they will be given about the Bible and not to let it infect them. As a result they leave college preaching exactly the same sermons as when they came in – sometimes literally so.

On the other side of the equation, there have been students who are so completely sold on the critical approach that they no longer see the Bible as an inspiration to faith but simply a tool to give us insights about the early Church, a window through which to see the first century, rather than a mirror in which to see ourselves. They would argue that a Bible where, according to critical scholarship, the story of the marriage feast of Cana is a literary and theological creation rather than an historical event or which contains a book which purports to come from Paul, but which wasn't written by Paul or which supports the subjection of women, or slavery, cannot be of any value for enhancing spiritual life. They attend the guild, but the Bible no longer has any spiritual value for them.

These, of course are the two extremes. A third approach is the schizophrenic one, and this is very common in our theological colleges. In this approach both critical scholarship and spiritual reading are held in tension. Critical scholarship is enjoyed for its own sake. Much time and enthusiasm is spent trying to find a solution to the Synoptic Problem or arguing about the value, or otherwise of the New Perspective on Paul. As an intellectual exercise it is exciting and stimulating and useful, allowing them to learn many transferable skills, always very desirable in a university setting when your teaching quality assessment comes along. Scholarly material is learned for the examination and treated as an academic exercise and kept in one compartment of the brain. In the other compartment, and completely separate from the former, is the understanding of the Bible as a challenge and an aid to leading a spiritual life. Here critical scholarship does not come in to it. The model of reading is very like that of the fresh convert who when asked about Bible study, says, 'I just open my Bible and God talks to me, and then I close the Bible and I talk to God'. In other words, critical studies are embraced for the examination and then basically forgotten. They add nothing to an application of the text.

A fourth approach is to take account of critical scholarship and all the insights found in the New Testament Guild but to pick and choose. To give some examples: many students will take on board Synoptic Criticism and study the two versions of the Lord's Prayer and notice how God is addressed in both versions in two different ways and use that as point of meditation on the nature of God, or on the two different tenses used in the petition about bread and use that as a way of meditating on faith and reliance on God in the Christian life. They will enjoy and use insights gained from a study of Middle Eastern culture (something I am very enthusiastic about, having lived in the Middle East) and read with great interest the many introductions to a sociological approach to the New Testament. They will also use the insights of narrative criticism, studying the way a story is put together, pointing out, for example, the punch line in so many parables where the unexpected statement makes the point. But they ignore other insights from critical scholarship which they see as destructive of the usefulness of the Bible for aiding spiritual growth – *e.g.*, the question marks over Paul's authorship of 1 Timothy and the impact that might have on our understanding of certain passages in it.

INTEGRATING THE CRITICAL AND THE SPIRITUAL

So, these are the kinds of questions I have been wrestling with throughout my 35 years of teaching, I have been looking for a model which would integrate more clearly a critical and a spiritual reading of the text. Does *lectio divina* help me in that? The answer is: without doubt, yes.

From the insights which I have gained, both from the theoretical, academic lectures, from the description of the practice of *lectio divina* in Brazil and Trinidad, and from the actual practice of it by Bishop Monari I would like to make a few comments.

Lectio divina has a real strength for me and my tradition in that it takes seriously the aspiration that our Bible study should lead us to an encounter with the living God rather than the acquisition of concepts and principles. As Boa puts is: it is formational reading (or as we heard in the conference transformational reading) rather than (I would like to say, as well as) informational reading. In the circles where I work the encouragement of the listeners to meditation, prayer, contemplation and action is a timely reminder of why we study the Scriptures in Church in the first place. *Lectio divina* lifts Bible study from being an arid academic or intellectual exercise to being a spiritual experience. It invites us to submit to the word, rather than control it.

Lectio divina has a real strength because it brings together insights developed over the years in the story of the Church, and presents them in an orderly manner. The congregations with which I work would probably find the Latin words *lectio, meditatio, contemplatio, oratio, consolatio, discretio, deliberatio* and *actio*, a little daunting and perhaps off-putting. But that is simply a linguistic problem and other suitable words could

be found such as reading, meditation, contemplation, prayer, consolation, discernment, transformation, action. We would pay attention
to the first two, reading (exegesis) and contemplation (application),
then prayer and finally action, but would have less knowledge of some
of the others. But the eight concepts allow one to look at the text from
every angle; and over a period of time would become second nature
rather than a list of things to do. Presumably , when that happens
and when the approach has been learned, it can be used much more
flexibly that simply following eight pointers.

It also has the strength of having the potential of being used in different forums: in formal preaching in a church; in community Bible
study groups and in personal, private settings. We heard a beautiful
presentation of the lectionary reading using *lectio divina*, but other
papers have shown that that is not necessarily or even most commonly
the way *lectio divina* is used. It is a communal activity as the people of
God spend time with the Word of God, as well, of course, as being very
personal and very individual.

ALLOWING THE TEXT TO SPEAK

This brings me to my final point: the *lectio*. This is the kernel of
lectio divina. I liked the phrase 'attentive reading', allowing the text
to speak to us but it is here that I think in my tradition we have to be
particularly careful.

We have had an example of a superb *lectio*, which opens up the
passage in a way that I found exciting and informative.[1] It took up
more than a quarter of the entire presentation. It was fresh, critically
respectable and informative. I loved it. *Lectio divina* done like that has
my complete and enthusiastic support.

However, in one description that I heard from a practitioner, he
suggested that *lectio divina* consisted of reading and re-reading the
passage until some thought jumps out at you. When that happens,
one then move on to *meditatio*. This, I think, is fine in a community
setting where through sheer numbers and the inspiration of the Holy
Spirit, there is the possibility that the message of the passage will be

---

1. See Luciano Molinari, '*Lectio Divina* and the Story of the Widow', pp. 102-115,
supra.

teased out. But, for example, in the setting of the preparation for the preaching of a sermon or even private meditation, simply reading and re-reading the passage would make me just a little bit nervous. I think that we could end up with the good Presbyterian phenomenon of a hundred texts but the same sermon – as we constantly find our hobby horses in the text.

Is this necessarily bad? Probably not if there are enough hobby horses! But it could be very limiting. People could find in the reading what they want to find, rather than what God wants them to find. Or again, could tell God what we want him to tell us. In presenting *lectio divina* or something like it to my students, I would want to linger on the *lectio* and make sure that exegesis was being done in an acceptable way. In this respect I would want to encourage my group to use the insights from critical scholarship as they are able. Critical scholarship is the lens through which we can see the first century more clearly and which helps to correct any astigmatism which may be impairing our vision. Practically speaking, probably what I am advocating is the fourth approach listed above: use what is important and relevant from critical scholarship and leave the hard questions to the academy. Don't throw the baby of critical scholarship out with the bath-water, but don't allow concern for academic problems to get in the way of meeting with the living God in Scripture. I think that it is interesting that this was an area covered very widely in almost all the talks.

Has my trip been worth while? Certainly! I have been inspired and helped and enthused to continue the wonderful privilege of encountering God in the Scriptures. But I have also been impressed by how close our two traditions now are in their efforts to read the Scriptures. I have always known how close New Testament scholars were in the New Testament Guild, but I am excited by how close parishioners, or at least the ones meeting in this conference, are as well. I think every issue which we discussed over the weekend would have been echoed in discussions in our tradition about Bible study. As I say, the vocabulary may, in fact would, be different but the concepts are the same. Is it not time, therefore, for an excellent centre such as this Dominican centre to set about a project for developing and encouraging *lectio divina* ecumenically?

Being True to the God of the Bible

✠ LUCIANO MONARI

IN HIS BOOK on religion in the contemporary world, *The Metamor-phoses of God*, sociologist Fréderic Lenoir presents the thesis that in contemporary world and culture religion hasn't disappeared at all. On the contrary, in some aspects it is thriving more and more. But it is undergoing a deep metamorphosis. The experience of the great historical religions gives way to a varied multitude of movements, sects, proposals, religious emotions, which try to answer different religious needs. Everyone builds a personal religion to cope with his/her personal problems. According to Lenoir, the novelty may be described as the passage from a personal God to an impersonal, religious mystery; from the Creator God who is transcendent and unequalled to a God identified with the world itself; from a transcendent and male God to an immanent and female divinity. Finally: from God to divine.

It isn't difficult to see that all these three trends are opposite to Hebrew and Christian revelation: according to biblical religion, God is a free subject, conscious of himself, who chose to come in search of humanity and to enter into alliance with it. It is evident that we are facing a difficult and decisive challenge. The problem is not to defend God who is perfectly able to defend himself and his glory. The problem is to defend man from false or partial images of God, images which could lead to a hidden form of slavery. Think of Jeremiah's words when, accusing Israel's idolatry, he says: 'They went after worthless things, and became worthless themselves' (Jer 2:5).

That is exactly what is at stake: the kind of divinity people worship

---

✠ Luciano Monari, a Vice-President of the Italian Bishops' Conference, has spoken on Scripture at the last three World Youth Assemblies. He studied under Cardinal Martini, and was invited to the Limerick conference on Cardinal Martini's recommendation.

is not a matter of indifference. As Saint Augustine said with utmost clarity, man becomes more and more similar to the God he chooses to adore: adoring the true God, he becomes God's image; but adoring inert gods he will become inert himself. The choice of adoring the true God or of adoring idols affects the individual human, making him grow in liberty and responsibility or depressing him into fear of the world and its threatening powers. Let us listen again to Jeremiah: 'Do not learn the way of the nations, or be dismayed at the signs of the heavens; for the nations are dismayed at them.' (Jer 10:2) To face this challenge we need sound theological reflection, but, first of all, a coherent religious life: personal, dialogical, responsible.

To stand before the supreme mystery of being (God) as if we were before an impersonal mystery means to urge man towards de-personalisation, a lesser conscience of himself, a lesser assumption of responsibility. The religion of the Word, on the other hand, proclaims with clarity that God is a personal subject and that God calls us by name. Before God we may stand only as persons who are conscious of themselves and who live a relationship I-Thou. It's true that God is not a 'person' in the same sense in which we are persons; but the difference between God and us has to be thought of as a deeper, richer personality, not an impersonality.

If God is identified with the soul of the world (*Anima Mundi*), a relationship with God will be the same as a relationship with nature. But this attitude leads to a 'magic' way of looking at the nature (the animism of primitive religions). Nature is beautiful, but it has no heart, no feelings, no responsibility. Nature doesn't love and is unable to forgive; it remains plainly indifferent towards every being. In the cult of nature there is a regress which, objectively, cancels the creative place of a living God in the life of faith.

The risk arises of an irresponsible religiosity. If God is nothing other than the profundity of my soul, there is a risk that I will see nothing except my face. Narcissism is a characteristic immaturity of our time and a self-centred religion would easily lead us into a self-centered life.

PURIFICATION

But it's not enough to contrast the two opposite visions, a biblical religion (personal, dialogical, active) to postmodern (or hypermodern, as Lenoir calls it) religiosity which is impersonal, cosmic, egocentric. It is necessary that our religious experience assume and purify and elevate the needs to which modern religiosity is trying to answer. But how?

A Truer Sense of God

First of all, I think, through a live consciousness of the 'mystery' of God's word. God's eternal Word, the Word which made heaven and earth, became flesh; it became human words, sounds, meanings, languages. God's Word came among us.

There is a risk in preaching this event, because people can reduce the Word to its worldly aspects (sound, meaning, images…) and forget its origin in God. It becomes necessary to acquire and nourish the sense of mystery of the Word. God speaks; the word has a human form but it remains a divine word in which God says and reveals himself. The infinite distance between the God who speaks and the human who hears, must be clearly felt. Let us recall Ezekiel's experience when he saw God's glory by the Chebar canal in Babylon: 'When I saw it, I fell on my face, and I heard the voice of someone speaking.' (Ezek 1:28) or Peter's experience before Jesus' revelation: 'Go away from me, Lord, for I am a sinful man.' (Lk 5:8)

Unfortunately, the historical and critical approach doesn't help much because it chooses to approach God's Word only from its human side. It's a possible sound methodological choice to look at the human form with a maximum of methodological correctness; but this approach doesn't exhaust the Word's mystery and its religious meaning.

A Truer Sense of the Human

We must stress also the importance of the human subject with all its experiences, ideas, images, hopes, desires, fears. It's true that God's word overcomes man's being, but it's also true that the I of the hearer is deeply involved; he is a real subject before God. Saint Augustine speaks of God as more inner in me then my inner self and higher in me than my highest self (*intimior intimo meo, superior summo meo,*). Of course Augustine doesn't fall into the danger of identifying God's being and man's deepths. Nevertheless he clearly feels that God is not simply outer to man; that in the encounter with God man reaches the real centre of his own personal mystery.

There is no opposition between the 'ego' of the person and the 'ego' of God; there is, on the contrary, a relationship which gives value to the person itself. If we want our experience of the word to be complete, we must make it resound in the deepth of the human heart. Let us remember an experience the Gospel of John mentions a few times: the experience of being known by Jesus. When Nathanael approaches the Lord and hears from him a revelation about his person, he asks: 'Whence did you come to know me?' A similar experience is narrated about the Samaritan woman or Mary of Magdala on Easter Day. To meet Jesus, God's Word made flesh, means not only to know God in a new way, but even 'to be known' by God. And that means, in a concrete way, to know oneself in a new way starting from God and from His word.

A Truer Sense of the World

And, finally, the cosmic dimension. It's not difficult to appreciate the importance of this dimension for modern men. We, moderns, feel a deep need of contact with nature, just because we have been removed from it by technology and industrial production. We know that a correct relationship with nature is necessary for our mental sanity. When this relationship fades, when humankind produces thoughts and ideas but is no more able to receive impressions, perceptions, sensible data from the outside world, mental balance staggers and we easily falls into depression.

The Bible proclaims that nature is 'God's creation' and so nature is a reality in which it is possible to contemplate the mystery of the Creator and the sense of the world. We read in Ps 104: 'Bless the Lord, O my soul. O Lord my God, you are very great. You are clothed with honour and majesty, wrapped in light as with a garment.' It's a contemplative perception of nature in which a reflection of God's beauty and glory shines.

Lenoir's view is that modern man needs a world enchanted anew and he supports this opinion by citing the success of the Harry Potter novels and films or the works of J. R. R. Tolkien. I don't know if this kind of magically enchanted world has a real consistency beyond its literary dimension. But I know well that a vision of the world as creation lets the symbolic dimension of reality be expressed clearly and greatly. We don't need elves or fairies to make the world full of meaning; it's enough to remember that a creature always reflects a Creator:

> The One who prepared the earth for all time filled it with four-footed creatures; he sends forth the light and it goes, he recalls it, and it obeys him, trembling; the stars shone in their watches and were glad; he called them, and they said: Here we are! They shone with gladness for him who made them. (Bar 3:32-35)

Facing the Challenge with Lectio Divina

We already have the instruments to answer with confidence to the challenge of hypermodern religiosity. We must learn to use these instruments in the arena of contemporary thought and imagination. The practice of *lectio divina* appears to be precious because it models our relationship with God in the correct way, helps us to become responsible persons before a personal, loving God.

> This was the appearance of the likeness of the glory of the Lord. When I saw it, I fell on my face, and I heard the voice of someone speaking. He said to me: O mortal, stand up on your feet, and I will speak with you. And when he spoke to me, a spirit entered into me and set me on my feet; and I heard him speaking to me. (Ezek 1:28–2,2)

The splendour of God's glory dazzles Ezekiel and presses him against the ground; but God's word lifts Ezekiel up and puts him before God as his partner. He is only a 'son of man' – a human being – but God's word makes him God's hearer. God's partner! Just so.

Coming in *Doctrine & Life* in 2010

Mary, the Clairvoyant and the Archbishop
Mary T. Malone

The Challenge of the ARCIC Agreement on Mary
Eoin de Bhaldraithe

Biodegradable Calvin
Ruth Whelan

What Can Theology Say to the Current Economic Crisis?
David Smith

'Global Woman': Capitalism and Distributive Justice
Maria Duffy

The State as Indirect Employer: an Irish Perspective from the Catholic Social Tradition
Tony McNamara

The Challenge of the New Spirituality
Jack Finnegan

A New Evangelisation: a New Emancipation for Ireland
Joe Egan

Appearing ten times a year, *Doctrine & Life* provides a forum to enable a dialogue between the inheritance of Christian faith and the concerns of today's world – political, artistic and economic. Its outlook is ecumenical as it analyses questions posed by current dilemmas and charts developments in Church life.